Please consult a licensed professional before attempting any techniques outlined in this book.

By reading this document, the reader agrees that under no circumstances is the author responsible for any losses, direct or indirect, that are incurred as a result of the use of information contained within this document, including, but not limited to, errors, omissions, or inaccuracies.

Table of Contents

Psychology 101

Learn How to Read Minds, Win People & Influence Anyone with Hypnotism, Deception and Covert Neuro-Linguistic Programming

Jay Laurson

Introduction

Welcome! In this book, you will learn the basics about the human brain and how the brain impacts human emotion and behavior. You will learn how the field of psychology developed and how it has changed over the centuries. Then you will learn about mind-reading, hypnosis, deception, and neuro-linguistic programming. You will see how these skills can impact and motivate others and how you can use them in both your personal and professional life, both openly and covertly. Through their use, you can both improve your own focus and stress-level, and also learn to better work with others and motivate them toward specific outcomes. You will learn to be a more savvy consumer, employer, employee and family member, learning how these techniques may be used on you, as well as by you.

The Human Brain

The human brain: approximately three pounds of matter that controls every part of the human existence. The brain controls bodily functions, emotions, thoughts, and every other part of keeping us alive.

How the human brain works and how it impacts human behavior continues to be one of the great mysteries of humanity. Humans have worked for centuries to try to understand how to change human behavior, and in some cases, how to manipulate human behavior for personal or organizational gain.

While people have tried to understand the brain since the beginning of human time, in the late 1480s, Leonardo DaVinci explored human brains during autopsies. He was looking to understand how the brain was constructed and how thoughts and emotions developed and interconnected. DaVinci was seeking knowledge, but as he did so, he kept countless drawings and diagrams of the brain and spinal column, sharing that knowledge with other scientists and doctors.

What do we know about the brain as an organ? We know that the brain grows with the body until it reaches full adult size. Males tend to have larger brains than females. Sixty percent of the brain is fat, meaning that it has the highest percentage of fat of any organ in the body. Research shows that having a larger brain does not mean someone is more intelligent (Mann, 2016).

What else do we know about the brain? What happens if it is injured? Can it heal itself? We know that the human brain can be injured and still function in some cases, or even heal itself. We know that a brain injury may take years or even decades to show its true impact, such as the brain deterioration shown later in life: for example, Chronic Traumatic Encephalopathy (CTE) in the brains of former National Football League players. We know that people on the autism spectrum tend to have physically larger brains than those not on the autism spectrum. We know all these bits of information about the human brain, yet it still largely is a mystery to us.

The human brain is a highly complex organism, divided into separate lobes or sections. Each section is its own very complicated system and is responsible for specific bodily functions, thoughts, emotions, speaking, vocabulary and motion.

The first, most animalistic section of the brain is the brain stem, which is responsible for the basic body functions. The brain stem keeps us breathing, swallowing and sleeping, and regulates body temperature and digestion. This is also the section of the brain that controls the "flight, fight or freeze" response in humans when they feel threatened. This tends to be proportionally larger in men than in women (Mann, 2016).

The second section is the cerebellum, which is responsible for balance and coordination. Then comes the occipital lobe, which controls our sight and perception of color. The parietal lobe is in charge of sensory responses, balance and coordination, reading, and spatial recognition.

The temporal lobe regulates behavior, memory, understanding of language, and hearing. The temporal lobe takes all of the auditory messaging around someone and makes sense of it for the brain. It is how we make meaning of the sounds around us.

The final lobe is the frontal lobe, which is responsible for regulating and understanding emotion, speaking, problem-solving, reasoning, and movement by choice (as opposed to reflex movement). The frontal lobe is proportionally larger in women than in men. This is the lobe of the brain that schools and universities try to engage early on to help students focus in school in order to access their learning.

Scientists now understand what each section controls, but they have also learned that the brain can adjust for missing parts, illness or injury. For example, there are examples of people who have received traumatic brain injuries in the frontal lobe, but over time, the brain has rewired itself, enabling the person to regain speech. The bridge between the hemispheres of the brain, the corpus callosum, normally provides the integration and communication between the parts of the brain, and doctors now know that with early intervention, babies born without the corpus callosum can rewire their own brains to work without that bridge. The human brain and its adaptability are just plain amazing!

The understanding of the human brain and the ways in which the brain controls both the body and emotions are still largely a mystery. Each day, the understanding of the human brain grows, but there is an almost infinite amount of learning still possible and needed. The more humans learn about the brain, the more questions about it arise, and the more complex and amazing it seems.

The techniques we are about to explore are behavioral strategies that can be used to access and motivate various lobes and sections of the brain.

Our Shared Learning

Mind-reading, hypnosis, deception and neuro-linguistic programming are all techniques used to understand human emotions, thoughts and behaviors. They also are used in order to change behavior or bring about specific outcomes. The changing of behavior may be because the subject wants to change their own reality, or it can be because someone else wants to bring about that change for their own reasons or purposes (Hunter, 2010). In this book, we will look at the origins and uses of each of these techniques, the pros and cons of each, and how they can be used both openly and covertly.

Chapter 1: Welcome to Psychology 101

Welcome to Psychology 101! This is a journey of self-awareness, learning, and understanding ourselves and those around us in our professional and personal lives. Just as if Psychology 101 was studied in college, in this book you will learn about the history of psychology, and then move on to the hot topics of mind-reading, hypnotism, deception, and open and covert uses of neuro-linguistic programming (NLP).

We will then move on to how to use these techniques both on yourself and on others, how they are used on each of us daily, and discuss the positive and negative aspects of using them in all situations.

The History of Psychology

We often hear the word psychology. What does it mean, and how did the study of psychology begin?

Psychology is the study of how the human mind works, how

emotions develop and manifest, and how human behavior is impacted and driven by those emotions. It is the study of how humans think.

Psychology is a very complex discipline that includes many subtopics, such as child development, attention and focus, attachment, obsessive behaviors, anger, addiction, sexuality, adolescent development, sports psychology, eating disorders, impact of adverse childhood experiences (trauma), organizational/systems theory, post-traumatic stress disorder, clinical psychology, the impact of mental health on physical health, social behavior, structural psychology, and cognitive behavioral responses. Each of these subtopics is a field of study in its own right, but for this book, we will not discuss or learn about the majority of them.

The study of psychology did not emerge as a separate and respected science until the late 1800s, primarily in Europe and North America. While all human civilizations have pondered human existence, the formal study of the brain and human emotion and behavior has been more prevalent in the Western societies, especially in the last two hundred years (Mann, 2016).

Long before the 1800s, the early Greeks started looking at the responses of humans in a variety of situations, trying to understand the cause and effect of each response. The Greeks looked at these situations through what is now recognized as philosophy, using logic and observation to explain the behaviors. In approximately 400 BC, Plato was writing about the human psyche, which he believed was the seat of all knowledge in a human. Plato stated that the brain held knowledge, which was a radical idea at the time. He believed that we have knowledge that we consciously know we have, as well as subconscious knowledge that we don't recognize is there (Mann, 2016). Plato postulated that with activating the psyche, humans could unlock that hidden or subconscious knowledge.

Plato's most famous student, Aristotle, took the theory of the psyche and embellished it and explored new theories. Aristotle wrote Para Psyche, which is considered the first book about psychology. Aristotle proposed that the body can only exist because the mind exists. He used his knowledge of zoology to connect the mind and body, and then proposed that there was a human soul which was the connection between current human existence and the divine. Aristotle explored human urges, including the urge to have sex and reproduce, and said that it was a connection between the mind and body. Aristotle also proposed that the human heart held emotion, and that the heart guides mental activity. While some of his theories were later found to be scientifically incorrect, his drive to understand emotions, urges and thoughts were revolutionary, and he was correct in his assertion of a mind-body connection.

Other later Greeks then proposed that the human mind and physical health were connected. They conducted many experiments, including vivisection (dissecting someone while they were still alive), to understand the body and nerves and how they connect to thoughts and emotions.

Around that same time, the philosopher and scientist Galen

proposed that the body has four humors, which he proposed were the emotions of a person. Galen believed that the humors needed to be aligned in order for someone to be healthy and happy. While his theory is now seen as erroneous, it was the first time that human behavior was clearly linked to the body in this way. This again was a revolutionary idea, as it was a move away from the widely accepted theory that behavior was linked to the presence and work of evil spirits, demonic possession or witchcraft. Galen's theories held that a person's behavior comes from within; not from outside spiritual forces.

It wasn't until much later in human history that there was a true move to what we now recognize as scientific research and methodology, which resulted in the development of the science of psychology. In the late 17th century, the French philosopher Rene Descartes started to wrestle with the mind and body being two separate parts of the whole of a person. This was referred to as dualism, and it was the true beginning of the science of psychology (Mann, 2016).

The study of the body, physiology, was also part of this progression. Early studies about the brain, and especially those relating to human behavior, combined in such a way that researchers began to recognize the need to study them separately from the body. They also recognized that while they could learn about the body from living humans, the brain was invisible in its physical form until after death. Posthumous dissection of the brain showed the forms, but doctors and scientists weren't able to see it functioning.

There were some early experiments and surgeries on the brain while the subject was still living, especially in drilling through the skull to alleviate pressure or the buildup of fluid. In a few horrible cases, doctors drilled through the skull while the person was alive, with the intent to allow evil spirits or negative forces to leave the brain. Those experiments and operations did give some information about the brain, most specifically about the fluids around it and how it healed after being exposed. They didn't give a lot of information about the inner workings of the brain, especially those pertaining to emotions, thoughts or motivations. Also, due to the fact that such procedures were incredibly painful and physically traumatic, the information gathered about brain function from them was tinged with pain and fear responses.

In 1848, one of the most important events in the history of brain research occurred. A laborer named Phinneas Gage was injured by an iron pole going through his skull and brain. The accident was bizarre, and to this day is still studied both as an industrial accident and for what doctors learned about the human brain because of it (Mann, 2016).

A misfiring of a charge while Gage was working on a rail project in Vermont led to a forty-three inch rod entering his head through his cheek, going through the frontal lobe of his brain, and then exiting his skull and landing feet away from him. Gage walked to a wagon and was taken to a local doctor, who said that he could actually see Gage's brain through the wounds. When Gage got sick to his stomach and vomited, pieces of his brain came out of the holes, and the horrified doctor collected them in a tea cup, unsure of what to do with the bits.

Gage survived, although there was a huge change in his personality. People who had known him his entire life said that the injury changed him permanently. It could be argued that just surviving such a horrific ordeal would have caused personality changes; however, it was found posthumously that the rod had destroyed much of his frontal lobe. It was nothing short of miraculous that he not only survived the accident, but lived for years after with only a personality change as the major outcome of the accident.

By studying Gage, doctors became increasingly convinced that different parts of the brain control different parts of thinking, speaking, bodily functions and emotions. Gage's injury and the learning within the scientific community because of his accident and subsequent survival, radically changed the knowledge of the human brain and opened up new sub-fields of brain research.

Years later, the physiologist Wilhelm Wundt wrote a book published in 1874. His book focused on how thinking and behavior connect, although Wundt's work at this time did not look at human emotion in any sort of depth. In 1879, Wundt opened the first program to study psychology at the University of Leipzig, denoting the first time that psychology reached this level of academic recognition and respect. In all, it is commonly reported that 17,000 students attended Wundt's lectures, showing the wide-spread acceptance of his work and the interest in the mind-body connection and psychology in general (Mann, 2016).

After Wundt's work, many of his students furthered the study of psychology. For example, Edward Titchener developed the theory of structuralism, in which psychologists would look at emotional and behavioral responses and try to break them down to the most basic parts of perception and sensation. William James then developed the theory of functionalism, in which the emphasis changed to look at how the understanding of behavior can help someone in their daily personal and professional life.

Then came the most famous of all the researchers in psychology, Sigmund Freud. Freud developed a theory about how the unconscious mind impacts every aspect of life. Freud believed that both childhood experiences and impulses coming from the unconscious contribute to the personality and behavior of adults.

Freud promoted the idea that these unconscious impulses eventually express themselves, often through dreams and verbal expressions referred to as "Freudian Slips," whereby comments show inner thoughts and feelings, often about uncomfortable topics such as sexual thoughts or feelings. While many of Freud's theories are no longer widely accepted by mainstream psychology experts, they still revere him as the father of psychological therapy and analysis, and he remains the most well-known psychologist or psychotherapist in human history.

To date, most Americans still think of the Freudian method of psychoanalysis as the current reality of counseling therapy. They picture the couch, with the client or patient reclining on it while an older man asks them detailed and pointed questions about their upbringing, toileting history and sexual thoughts. In the Freudian method, the analyst is emotionally detached from the patient, looking for specific patterns and history to address, and is very controlling of the process. In truth, very few Freudian psychoanalysts still are in practice, and counseling is no longer as scripted or detached as it was during Freud's time.

In the beginning of the 20th century, psychology changed again, focusing on the theory of behaviorism (Mann, 2016). Behaviorism was a theory developed primarily by Ivan Pavlov, most well-known for his experiments with dogs, who he trained using their desire for edible treats. Pavlov celebrated and shared the idea that behavior could be changed and manipulated by conditioning and stimulus.

While many other psychologists, such as John Watson, embraced the behaviorist movement, one stood above the rest: B.F.Skinner, who was a researcher and professor at Harvard University. Skinner became the newest expert, showing that behavior could be changed and manipulated through rewards (reinforcement) and punishment. Many schools developed their behavior protocols based on the work of Skinner. For example, the use of token reward systems is still in wide-spread use in schools as a way of monitoring and controlling students' behaviors.

Within Western society, many primary and elementary schools have adopted systems such as Response to Intervention (RTI) and Positive Behavioral Interventions and Supports (PBIS), which are based largely on Skinner's work. In those systems, all students are taught the same basic behavioral skills and are rewarded through a token/reward system for good behavior. These systems are built on the idea that the desire for those rewards will motivate the students struggling with behavior to act the right way.

Interestingly, current research shows that this only works with children who have normal social and emotional development; not with children who have experienced trauma or have endured many adverse life experiences. The research shows that using Skinner's ideas of rewards with children who have experienced trauma without having the healing brought about by therapeutic intervention will actually make them less likely to act appropriately, thus casting some overall doubt on Skinner's theories and their implementation.

After behaviorism, psychology arrived at humanistic psychology, in which there was an emphasis on conscious experiences. Carl Rogers from the United States has been recognized as the leader in this school of thought. Rogers believed strongly in the power of self-determination and personal (free) will. This was an important change in the world of psychology, as the theory of free will emphasizes that humans make conscious decisions about their behavior rather than that it is predetermined. This allows for the idea that behavior can be changed if the motivation is there.

Abraham Maslow also then joined the field of humanistic psychology, developing the theory of the hierarchy of needs and suggesting that those needs impact the behavior of people. For example, Maslow believed that if the most basic needs (food, shelter, etc.) were not provided for people, their behavior would be in line with seeking to fulfill those needs. A child who is hungry will do anything to get food. Maslow also believed and promoted the theory that if the basic needs are met, humans can then focus on higher level needs and more intellectual pursuits.

In the 1950s and 60s, a new field of psychology developed, and it continues to grow and change even today. That was the field of cognitive psychology. In this field, there was a reduction in the emphasis on psychoanalysis and behaviorism, and instead the focus was placed on the connection between behaviors that can be observed and what is happening emotionally for the person. In the study of cognitive psychology, researchers and therapists focus on perception, use of language, memory, attention, creativity and problem-solving (Mann, 2016).

In the study of cognitive psychology, researchers have moved into studying how humans make decisions, how language forms and is used, how decisions are made and problems are solved, and how memory and perception work and influence human behavior. This has allowed for the explosion of counseling practices based upon identifying the issue, setting goals with the client, and moving them through both talk counseling and behavioral change. Cognitive psychology also stresses a cause-effect relationship, such as unidentified or treated feelings of self-loathing leading to over-eating.

As science and technology has improved and changed, technologies such as magnetic resonance imaging (MRI) and positron emission tomography (PET) scans have allowed for new learning about the brain and how the physiology and pathology of the brain impacts human health and mental health/behavior.

The emergence of brain technologies that allow doctors and researchers to look at brain function in a living human are causing a huge and rapid growth in the knowledge and understanding of the human brain. For example, prior to the emergence of the MRI and PET scan technologies, doctors had to look at brains post-mortem in autopsies. Only in rare cases could doctors see a brain working, such as in surgical situations. Now, doctors and researchers can observe the brain in living humans not under anesthesia, leading to greater and greater understanding and knowledge. Specifically looking at the role of PET scans, they can detect hot spots in the brain that show possible pathology, and see what parts of the brain react or don't react to stimuli.

Now that a basic history of psychology has shown how the field has evolved to its current understanding of the connection between the brain and emotions, emotions and physical health, and the mind-body connection overall, it is time to look at ways in which psychology can be used to guide and shape interactions with others. Specifically, we will be looking at mind-reading, hypnosis, deception and NLP. In the case of

NLP, we will be learning about both the open use of NLP and the covert use of it, often referred to as conversational hypnosis. In later chapters, we will look at each topic in depth, both in terms of the development of the strategies and practice, specifics in how to use them, ethical dilemmas, and how you can learn more about them.

Mind-Reading, Hypnosis, Deception, and NLP

As noted, this book explains the history and use of the techniques of mind-reading, hypnosis, deception and neuro-linguistic programming. In this chapter, there is a brief definition of each of these techniques before we move on to chapters addressing each in greater depth.

What is mind-reading? Mind-reading is the ability to intuit what others are thinking about at a given time. It relies most heavily on non-verbal communication skills and empathic intuition to be able to make an educated guess about what someone is thinking and feeling. While the skills can be learned and practiced on almost anyone, they are most effective on people you know well. As we will see, there are some people who, due to other issues or diagnosis, it may be almost impossible to mind-read, as their minds work differently to most people's.

Hypnosis is the induction of a trance-like state of deep safety and relaxation in which a person becomes more responsive to suggestions, whether about behavior or personal beliefs. The person hypnotized does not lose control of their body or mind, but they are more open to suggestions from others and more able to focus on problem-solving their own issues.

Deception is using lies, misleading information or omissions to cause reactions in others in order to change or motivate behavior. Deception can be practiced without the knowledge of others or in conjunction with them in systems-based deception. In deception, misleading behavior may be sporadic, only one time, or systematic over a long period of time.

NLP is a technique in which the patterns of thought in successful people are articulated and communicated, and people can practice the skills and patterns shared in order to bring about the achievement of personal or organizational goals. In open neuro-linguistic programming, practitioners work with the subject on understanding their own perception of reality and then set goals and develop a plan to achieve those goals. In covert neuro-linguistic programming, also known as conversational hypnosis, the subject or subjects do not know that their emotions and thought processes are being accessed in order to achieve the goals of someone else: for example, the goals of a group or organization.

Why Do You Want to Learn These Techniques?

At their heart, all of these techniques have the common purpose of looking to change, motivate or manipulate the behavior of oneself or others. By learning the techniques, we can all learn more about how our own brains work, and also focus more fully on how to work with others. Each of these techniques involves an understanding of oneself and others, and an understanding of the goals we each have. They can be used to help move our own personal agendas forward, or they can be used to work within and advance the progress of organizations or companies.

The techniques used primarily in mind-reading, hypnosis and neuro-linguistic programming all use empathy, observation and understanding of verbal and non-verbal communication, understanding of human motivation, systems theory, and interpersonal skills as a basis. All of them can help us understand ourselves and others better, and as leaders and employers, can help us motivate our staff to achieve their greatest potential. Deception can also be used to motivate behavior, although its use is controversial and potentially problematic if the deceit is uncovered.

Why would you want to use these techniques? Both the knowledge and skills you develop will help with your understanding of others in all situations. These techniques can also improve your romantic relationships and your work environment, help with sales and marketing, and help you gain advantage, therefore helping you to achieve your goals.

In this book, we will look into the research and basis of each of these techniques, talk about how you can learn to practice these skills effectively, and what the positive and negative ramifications of using them can be.

Chapter 2: What Is Psychology Now?

Now that the history of the development of the field of psychology has been explained in a very brief manner, showing the major early fields of thought and how they shifted and changed over the decades, now it is time to look at where psychology is today and see how it connects with mind-reading, hypnosis, deception and neuro-linguistic programming.

How Has Psychology Changed?

In today's terms, we now integrate psychology into every aspect of our professional and personal lives. While Freud's psychoanalysis has been widely discontinued as a practice, every county in the United States now has a public mental health counseling agency. Many public schools have on-staff mental health practitioners. We now train pediatricians and physicians for adults to look for signs of issues with mental health, and doctors regularly screen for depression and anxiety. The mind-body connection is now widely accepted, and more and more mental health diagnoses show the connection between psychological health and physical health.

The acceptance of psychology and the emergence of counseling services as an accepted part of self-care has exploded since the 1960s. Every public school in the United States now has connections to mental health agencies or has a clinician or school counselor on staff for assessment and treatment of mental health or behavioral issues in children. Of late, most schools in the United States also embrace the idea of trauma-informed or trauma-sensitive responses, looking for ways in which to support the most vulnerable students in a way that is appropriate and supportive, and no longer ostracize students.

Especially important in that trauma-sensitive approach is the understanding and practice that the mind and body are constantly connected, even when we can't see the connection. For example, educators are being trained to identify and understand the non-verbal cues associated with a child who has endured trauma in order to be better able to reach and educate the child. This more holistic approach, focusing on reading cues and responding in a proactive instead of reactive manner, is greatly helping vulnerable children to access their learning and be open to working on healing from their pasts. Schools have also found that this trauma-sensitive focus helps adults work together better and helps schools be more responsive and welcoming to all families.

Search agents on the Internet have also increased the accessibility of information about the brain, psychology, mental health, and the mind-body connection. This access to information is potentially both a good and bad thing. For example, searching the term "anxiety disorders" on Google brings over 223 million responses in less than a second. This huge amount of information may mean that the searcher understands that he or she is not alone in struggling with anxiety, but it may also lead to inaccurate self-diagnosis and potentially lead to treating the wrong ailment.

More and more people are self-assessing and self-diagnosing using the Internet, with varying degrees of success. While there are many outstanding resources about psychology online, there are also many sites that have inaccurate information. Especially problematic is the surge in online suppliers of medication to treat mental health issues, leading to people self-diagnosing and prescribing. Not only is the diagnosis possibly incorrect; it is done without counseling as a co-occurring treatment, and the medications are not regulated, controlled or monitored. Many of the sites online promote themselves as experts in mental health and behavioral motivation and control, and are also selling self-help products. The problem with the wave of supposed experts is that many very vulnerable people are taking their recommendations as expert advice and making mental and physical health decisions without full knowledge or true expertise, and without the correct follow-up from doctors or psychologists.

How Do the Topics of Mind-Reading, Hypnosis, Deception, and NLP Connect with Psychology Now?

Now that we have looked at how psychology has changed over the centuries, it is time to look at how the topics of mind-reading, hypnosis, deception and neuro-linguistic programming connect to modern psychology. Are they in alignment with current views and practices, or have they been largely debunked? Are they true psychological techniques or party tricks?

Both mind-reading and hypnotism are widely used in pop culture. They come from a long-standing tradition called mentalism, in which practitioners use simple techniques to understand others and control their behavior, often for the purpose of amusing others and as a means of earning income as a performer. The practicing of the mentalist arts is most frequently seen in entertainment, and is therefore often minimized or trivialized in terms of its actual value as a tool. Mentalists primarily create illusions so that their audiences believe they have supernatural powers, when instead they are very observant and able to tap into the vulnerabilities and issues of others. For example, think of the number of times they are used as a part of a show or movie, or in local events such as fairs. There are also many examples of mentalism being used as entertainment, where the performer uses a companion or associate to help create an illusion and fool the audience.

Mind-reading? A mind reader is a person who can supposedly tell what another person is thinking. Does this mean that the person uses telepathy to know what someone else is thinking? No, it does not. Mind-reading is the ability to make an educated guess about another's thoughts by using means other than our normal five senses of touch, hearing, sight, smell and taste. It is about non-verbal communication and being observant. It is about reading non-verbal cues such as body language. For example, it doesn't take an advanced degree in psychology to sense that someone is angry with you if the person is standing there tapping one foot, with their arms crossed and a huge scowl on their face. This form of mind-reading is not telepathy; instead, it is making educated and informed guesses based on what the mind-reader can see and hear.

What, then, is hypnosis? Again, there are many gags about making people quack like a duck by hypnotizing them. Every fair or circus has a hypnotist who promises to hypnotize members of the audience. Is this a real science or a trick? Basically, hypnotism is helping a person to reach a state of deep relaxation in which their brains become more open to suggestions about behavior or to exploring events from the past, and helping them become more able to problem-solve. Therefore, hypnotism can be used for entertainment, and people may enter a state in which they will act uncharacteristically. On the other hand, it can be used therapeutically to retrieve experiences, such as a traumatic event, or to change behavior, such as reducing the urge to eat or smoke cigarettes.

As a caveat, people can learn to self-hypnotize as a means of self-calming, or they can learn to hypnotize others, but this should not happen without the proper training and safety structures around it. For example, creating a situation in which someone will dance a waltz whenever a dog barks should not be left open-ended so that it might happen anywhere other than a specific entertainment venue. Similarly, practitioners have the moral imperative to not guide others to negative or self-harming behaviors, such as if they know that someone has anorexia and wants hypnosis in order to not eat. Hypnotism can be an exceedingly powerful tool, both in terms of motivation and creativity, and as a tool for changing behaviors, and thus needs to be used wisely, purposefully and carefully.

Now that the basics of mind-reading and hypnotism are clear, it is time to move on to deception and NLP. As we look at neuro-linguistic programming, we will differentiate between open uses of NLP and covert uses.

Deception in psychological terms is the same as it is in any other part of the human existence. It is the act of willingly and knowingly misleading someone about a situation, person, or your own self and behaviors. It is used to get information about someone when the person might be hesitant to share that information, and it can also be used to manipulate others and to improve the standing of the person practicing the deception.

NLP differs from deception. It is the study of how perception, communication and choices impact the human condition, and it promotes the idea that each person can make positive life changes. Covert neuro-linguistic programming focuses on perception and communication, but may be used to manipulate the behavioral choices of the subject in order to help the practitioner achieve their own goal or purpose.

Mind-reading, hypnosis, deception and neuro-linguistic

programming all rely on observation, non-verbal communication and an understanding of psychology, and others can change or manipulate that behavior if they have the skills and knowledge.

How are they used most often in society? They are used most frequently in intelligence communities, education, spying, marketing, and in self-help programs or products. All of us have other people trying to read our minds, hypnotize us, and motivate and change our behaviors to fulfill the needs and goals of others or of organizations every moment of the day. Knowing that this is a constant part of our world helps us be aware and make sure that we are not vulnerable to negative influences, while also understanding how we can use the tools to improve our own lives.

Chapter 3: Mind-Reading

Think back to being a teenager. Once you get over the visceral response to remembering the intensity of emotions from that time in your life, close your eyes for a moment. Picture yourself in your favorite outfit when you were 15; remember what you looked like, how your hair was cut; what you liked to eat each day. Remember your friendships and what mattered to you at that age. What did your backpack look like? Your school locker? Put yourself back in that body and mindset.

Now visualize yourself sitting at the lunch table in your high school. The sun is shining through the windows, and you are sitting with a couple friends, cafeteria trays in front of you. You stare across the cafeteria at the person you desperately want to date. You sit with your grilled cheese sandwich and tomato soup, begging the universe to let you know what the object of your affection is thinking. Do they like you too? If you asked them out, would they say yes? You sit there, wishing you could read minds like the person you saw on television. You stare at your crush's every move. Do they look over at you? Do you see a smile or a grimace? Are they showing warmth in their body language as they look at other young people, or is their body language saying that they want to leave that table or at least be on their own? What can you learn from their non-verbal cues? What can you tell about their interests by observing their behaviors and conversations? How much easier your social life would be if you could read their mind!

Can you learn to read minds? Yes, you can. Read on to learn

how.

What Is Mind-Reading?

As discussed previously, mind-reading is being able to figure out what another person is thinking by observing their non-verbal communication. It is reading body language, facial expressions, skin coloration, eye movement, and so many other non-verbal cues. It relies on one's ability to notice small cues or changes, such as a sudden blush when a topic is raised, arms being crossed, how someone's head is being carried, or how someone sits. Does someone look down at the ground when talking to a work supervisor? That would suggest nerves or subservience.

All humans, unless they are specifically trained to not give easily readable cues or have one of the disorders that skews non-verbal communication, give off information about their thoughts and emotions every moment of every day. Mind-reading is taking that non-verbal information and combining it with what you hear a person say, what you know about them otherwise and what you know about the situation, and combining all of that information into a complete package of knowledge about that person.

Being able to read minds is a gift, but it is a gift that anyone can learn. Many of us are convinced that our loved ones should be able to read our thoughts all the time, but unless they have learned the skills, they may not be successful at intuiting what we are thinking. Many couples who have been together for a long time claim to be able to read the mind of their partner, and truly, as they have been knowingly or unknowingly learning about the person for so long, they probably can "read" that mind pretty well and consistently. Often, couples who have been happily together for many years will appear to complete each other's thoughts and statements.

How do you read someone's mind? Why would you want to? In many movies, mind-reading is for evil-doing. If the bad guy can read the heroine's mind, he can find out where the fortune is hidden, right? In reality, the ability to identify and understand what someone else is thinking will help with interpersonal relationships. Even with strangers, practicing the skills can help prevent misunderstandings, help develop relationships, and help you achieve your goals.

Imagine this: you are on a cruise ship on a vacation with your partner. When you aren't on vacation, you shy away from desserts, wanting to control your weight. On vacation, you let yourself splurge. So, after a brisk walk around the deck, you go for a treat to reward yourself for getting that exercise. Patiently, you wait in the dessert line. You get to the counter, and there is only one small bowl of chocolate mousse left. That bowl of mousse looks so very good. You can't wait to sit down and take a spoonful of it, and you plan to savor every morsel. Suddenly, the woman behind you makes a sad sound as your hand reaches toward the bowl. You turn to look at her, your mother's lectures about manners echoing in your head. You ask, "Would you like it?" The woman says "No," and then takes a deep and sad breath and sighs, still looking longingly at the treat.

In that moment, you have a choice to make about your own behavior. You could go with her head shake and comment, and eat that bowl of mousse yourself. But deep down, you recognized the non-verbal cues that said she really wanted it. You took her eye movement of looking longingly at the treat and her sigh, and put that information together so that you realized that even as she verbally said she didn't want the mousse, she really did want it. You recognized that her saying no reflected her doing what she thought was socially acceptable and was not how she truly felt.

If you honor that communication you gathered through your mind-reading abilities, you hand over the mousse with a smile and probably have a new friend. That woman will walk away, amazed that someone knew how she felt, even as her verbal statement contradicted her non-verbal cues.

At its heart, mind-reading is a highly developed form of non-verbal communication, and in this increasingly technological world, humans are spending less and less time on direct person-to-person verbal communication, instead moving toward more electronic communication. How often do you just respond to a text message with either a one word text or an emoji? How often do you communicate using texting, DMs or email instead of in-person conversation or phone calls? As we use technology more and more, we lose the skills honed over centuries for reading minds because even though we are now in constant communication with the people in our lives, very little of it is face-to-face communication, and therefore it is difficult to read their non-verbal cues.

Even with those technological adaptations, we attempt to read the minds of others constantly through their communications via digital means. How often have you tried to intuit the emotion behind a text or email, or been convinced someone was angry with you because a message was short, when instead it was just that the person was busy at that moment? How often do we think someone is upset because of using caps in a message, when it may have just been that the Caps Lock key was on? How often do we text the wrong person because we are in a hurry? In all of these electronic communications, we are moving away from face-to-face human interaction or a conversation over distance through a phone call, and instead we try to understand emotions and thought patterns when the thoughts or statements go through electronic means.

We constantly make what we feel are educated guesses about how other people feel or will respond, whether in face-to-face, electronic, or other types of interactions. If we are truly tuned into their feelings and understand their non-verbal cues, we can do it with far greater accuracy. Those people with highly developed empathy will be more successful, as they can more quickly understand the feelings of others and put themselves in their shoes.

This ability to understand verbal and non-verbal communication of others and to understand motivation and responses can also be incredibly helpful to you as a leader or in other ways in your professional life.

How to Read Minds

Almost anyone can learn to read minds. Unequivocally, the best way is to start with someone you know, as it makes it more likely that you will be successful. Reading a stranger is possible, but it is much more difficult.

Starting with someone you know pretty well, look at their verbal communication over time. What tone do you hear? The choice of words? Volume? Do you see alignment in those areas? For example, does the person shout only when angry, or do they shout anytime they are excited? Does the choice of words and vocabulary change with emotion or situation? A perfect illustration of this is a person who only swears when they're angry. If you suddenly hear obscenities even when the person otherwise seems calm, you might need to look more deeply at their emotional state. Once you have started there, look for body language and other behavioral cues, always keeping in mind that gender, upbringing, culture and other factors impact body language and behavior.

The steps below are intended for use both with open and covert mind-reading. If you are doing this process openly, then be clear with the person about each step, so that they can understand and learn from the process as well. If you are doing it more covertly as a means of getting to know or motivate the person without specifically announcing that you're trying to read their mind, then practice the steps without that formal prior explanation.

First, practice your own mindfulness. Mindfulness is knowing and understanding our own bodies and emotions. It is being able to identify and control our own responses to stimuli. Learning these skills may come from meditation, yoga or other mindfulness-increasing practices. You will need to practice them regularly and with fidelity, and pay attention to your own mind and body. If you aren't centered in your own body and mind, your own internal white noise will block your ability to tune in to the feelings of others. Simply put, don't attempt mind-reading when agitated or upset. An open mind and open heart will greatly improve your ability to read others.

Next, truly focus on the person you want to read. As noted above, starting with people you know well may increase your success rate. Focus intently on them. Close your eyes, and picture them in your mind. What do their physical characteristics and mannerisms look like? Think about everything you have ever noticed about the person as an individual and what you know about their responses. When have you seen or heard the person act in an uncharacteristic way? What triggered that change of behavior? Think about how your own body and mind respond to their energy. Step back from what you outwardly recognize as your emotions when you are with the person, and instead recognize how your body (and internal energy) responds to theirs. Do you get in a room with the person and feel your own body reacting with anxiety, or do you feel a sense of calmness or optimism? How do they make you feel? You need to identify your own responses in order to be able to sift through them to the thinking of the person you're trying to read.

Now, if you haven't already done so, be in the same physical space with the subject, and try to have as few distractions around you as possible. Trying to read someone's mind in a crowded bar with a band playing and flashing decorative lights will be difficult due to the amount of distractions around you. Try to keep the environment as simple and distraction-free as possible.

Make and maintain eye contact for 15 seconds — no less; no more. More than that amount of time, and they will find you creepy and not want to be near enough for you to read their mind. Less than that, and you don't get a clear read on their energy and emotional state. Focus on what you can see physically about that person in terms of their body language and other non-verbal cues. Know that this eye contact may be exceedingly difficult for some subjects and that it may irritate them. Again, this is a good way to learn about your subject. Close your own eyes briefly after this eye contact, and picture the person and their energy in your own mind. See how you feel when you see that mental imagery, as often you will have subconsciously picked up cues from them already.

After the eye contact, start a conversation. Fixed answer questions close the brain down to more intuitive patterns of thought. For example, asking, "Did you eat lunch?" is a fixed answer question, with the answer simply being "Yes" or "No." The brain is less open to suggestion and openness when closed or fixed answer questions are used. Move to asking open-ended questions that are relatively neutral. Such questions and the subsequent answers will teach you a lot about your subject. Ask questions such as, "What did you do today?" or "What are your plans for the weekend?" The human brain becomes less guarded with open-ended questions, thus making it easier to read the thoughts or emotions of the subject.

Once you have started with open-ended questions, then move on to establishing a deeper rapport with your subject. How do you develop a deeper rapport? As uncomfortable as it feels, try using many of the same techniques as the police use in interrogations. Start by developing a connection by finding common ground. For example, if you know the person you want to read was born in Massachusetts like you were, use that as the start of a common connection. That simple commonality will be the start of a relationship between the two of you. You can continue that connection by using body language that shows you care, such as leaning forward, making eye contact and smiling. All of those non-verbal cues will also relax the subject and allow them to focus more fully on the conversation. When a person is less guarded because they feel a connection between you, you will use both the conversation and the non-verbal cues to read what they are thinking and feeling.

In that development of rapport, you need to have an open conversation and also be receptive to your own feelings about and responses to the person you are trying to read. Let yourself be open to the emotions and energy swirling around, even if your own body perceives them as negative or frightening. You need to allow the good and bad to flow your way so that you can then make your own meaning of their energy and non-verbal cues.

Following these steps, you can tap into what the other person is thinking about and can "read" their mind. If you are struggling with this, work on better understanding human emotions and motivation, and work on your listening skills. Do you listen in order to respond to someone or just to listen? Most people only listen enough to be able to argue or express their point; not because they want to better understand another human being.

Practice active listening. Practice just listening to another person talking, without interjecting your own opinion or recommendations: it will amaze you how much you learn when you just stop and listen to others instead of trying to get them to listen to you. It is an especially important skill to learn for interpersonal familial relationships, as often the people we care about the most only want us to listen — not respond, not answer, not try to solve the issue — just listen with an open heart and mind.

As part of this active listening, it also may be helpful to ask the person speaking if they want you to just listen, respond, suggest responses or resolutions, or solve the issue for them. Listen, ask, and follow their recommendations. It is imperative that you follow the request, as having someone be vulnerable enough with you that they feel safe to share with you means that they are trusting you fully. Don't abuse that trust by saying you will just listen and then try to solve the issue afterwards. Honor their feelings, even if it goes against your inner urges, as long as no harm will come to them or others by just listening.

Step by step, here is a summary of how to read minds:

- Step one: Decide who you want to read and why. What are you trying to learn from the person? What is your goal in reading that person's mind? Is there any downside to doing so, and if so, is it worth it?

- Step two: Be aware of your own mind-body connection. Are you centered in your own body? Are you calm and focused? Are you distracted by outside forces? Focus on how your own body feels and what emotions you are experiencing. Practice your own mindfulness. As discussed previously, if you aren't centered yourself, you won't be able to tune in to the feelings of others.

- Step three: Truly focus on the person you plan to read. Reflect on everything you have ever noticed about the person. What triggers them? What makes them laugh? What non-verbal cues do they give when agitated or in an emotional state? How do they act when calm and happy? Close your eyes and picture the person in your mind. Focus on that mental image.

- Step four: Find a distraction-free environment in which to read the person's mind, and then make eye contact with them for 15 seconds. Keep in mind that if this is being done completely covertly, it may be difficult to have eye contact in this way.

- Step five: Start a conversation, moving from fixed answer questions to open-ended ones, reading their reactions and establishing rapport. Find commonalities or connections to make a connection with the person. Where you are from, favorite foods, music, movies, sports and pets are all topics where you can usually find a common thread with someone.

- Step six: Move toward the topic you want to know about, and begin to ask questions or invite conversation about it. Listen for tone of voice. Watch for skin tone changes. Watch their eyes for signs that their concentration is waning. Pay attention to the verbal conversation, while also truly focusing on the person's non-verbal communication.

- Step seven: Intuit their thoughts on the topic based on their reactions to the conversation.

- Follow-up: Use the information you gleaned toward your goal. Focus on making good use of that information. Continue to use these steps with the subject, and you will continue to learn about the person.

Can all minds be read? Can all people learn to read minds? The answer is no to both questions. Many mental health diagnoses or other issues cause abnormal social responses or a lack of expected responses. Therefore, it is much more difficult — or even impossible — to read those minds. The most common example is people who are on the autism spectrum, who will usually struggle both to read minds and to be read. Because of their difficulty in understanding and reading verbal and nonverbal cues, their responses may not fit what is expected, and this makes them difficult to read. This difficulty in reading cues also means that people on the autism spectrum tend to be hesitant about having their minds openly read, as the concept of such interpersonal communication may be very difficult for them to grasp.

Many people who have diagnoses that impact the reading of social cues are taught by what is called scripting. In scripting, people are taught the socially acceptable response to situations and practice the response over and over. While they can usually replicate the scripted behavior, it may not be an indication of their true feelings or inner thought process. For example, children on the autism spectrum are often taught through scripting that the socially acceptable response to the question, "How are you?" is, "I'm fine. And you?" The child may not feel fine, but scripting teaches children to respond in that manner. Scripting is helpful as it allows for interpersonal interactions that might not have happened otherwise, but the interactions may seem forced or false due to the very consistent and expected response script.

Fast forward to adulthood, and those same individuals may not exhibit emotions or non-verbal cues in a way that is expected, or their true responses may be completely masked. Those adults may verbally state feelings or thought patterns based upon what they think others want from them, and what is expressed may or may not be their true feelings. Another issue in this is the difficulty in identifying true emotions when your perceptions of them may be different to those of the majority of people.

Therefore, know the person you want to read well enough to know if mind-reading is likely to work with them. Even if you won't be successful in actually reading that person's mind, you can still learn so much by observing behavior, responses and communication, and no matter what, your learning will help you work better with that person, whether in a personal or professional setting.

Pros and Cons of Mind-Reading

The first positive aspect of mind-reading is that the reader cares enough about the thoughts and emotions of the subject to want to know what they are thinking. That level of interconnectedness is increasingly rare. Mind-reading also takes a great deal of empathy and understanding of human emotion and cognition, and relies on the ability to read and understand non-verbal skills and communication. That is all positive and potentially helpful.

The potentially negative aspects to mind-reading come from the reader's ability to manipulate the emotions of others by claiming to know what they are thinking or feeling. It can also be used to take advantage of people who are vulnerable and are therefore letting down their guard more than normal. For example, visualize a situation where a young woman has just run away from home. She is waiting in a bus station, and someone unscrupulous who has this training and ability comes over to her and follows the steps to gain her trust. That person can read enough of what is going on in her inner turmoil to convince her to go with him into an unsavory situation or be convinced to try drugs. In a professional situation, it can be used to figure out the areas of vulnerability of a competitor, and then the person using the skills can manipulate a colleague or the situation overall.

What Do Skeptics Say?

What about those who claim to read minds of complete strangers in public situations? Are those claims real? While there are some people who claim, with some evidence, to be able to sense things about someone (such as psychics or mediums), in most cases, it is just excellent use of open-ended questions that can give enough information that someone feels they are being read in an intimate way.

For example, such a mind-reader (in a public event) starts off with, "I feel that you have lost someone." Immediately, people in the audience will start nodding, since most adults have lost at least one person they have cared about in their lives. By adding details like, "That person wants you to know that you are loved," the mind-reader has the hall filled with sniffling people, all feeling that their beloved grandma loves them. This is using open-ended questions or statements that have a high likelihood of having people identify with the comments as a tool to develop rapport. Then, once a verbal or non-verbal response occurs, the mind-reader can use that information to ask more questions and continue mining the audience for information while creating the impression of having a mysterious power.

Skeptics say that mind-reading is nothing more than making educated guesses based on body language and knowledge of the subject. But even the skeptics state that by focused observation of non-verbal cues and active and empathic listening, you can make detailed and usually accurate guesses about what someone is thinking (Navarro, 2015).

How Can Mind-Reading Be Used in a Work Setting?

How is mind-reading used in a professional sense or setting? We all know about the use of mind-reading techniques as they apply to police interrogation. The police use their knowledge of a situation and the information gathered through evidence, and add it to reading body language and non-verbal cues, along with active listening, in order to make educated guesses about what a suspect is thinking.

But in what other ways can mind-reading be used? The same techniques are often used by supervisors as they work with their employees. They are used to find ways in which to understand how their employees feel about a situation but also how to motivate them. For example, a supervisor in a restaurant sees that one waiter really shines when they're waiting on tables with families with young children, but struggles with tables where an older man is drinking excessively. The employer follows the steps outlined earlier, and through the open-ended questions and what he has learned from the waiter's behavior and the non-verbal cues picked up during the mind-reading, the employer realizes that the waiter has a past history of a parent drinking. That knowledge allows the employer to approach the situation from a supportive stance, offering his observations in a non-judgmental way, and therefore help the waiter feel supported and understood rather than defensive and defeated.

In a more negative light, such skills and practices may be used to manipulate employees. It can also be very useful for trying to achieve an advantage over a client or a competitor by seeing how they react non-verbally and verbally in conversations. Body language, skin coloration and other non-verbal cues show us how someone feels and show both areas of strength and areas of vulnerability. For example, using that same scenario with the waiter, if the employer has an issue with that waiter, once the employer has followed the steps of mind-reading, he could use the knowledge gained to put the waiter into situations that he knows would cause anxiety and stress, and could potentially lead to the employee leaving the job.

As discussed, the power of mind-reading can be enormous. At its most basic, the skills needed to read minds help with self-knowledge and interpersonal interactions. The more anyone knows about how others think and act, the better.

Chapter 4: Hypnosis

In the last chapter, you started by visualizing yourself as a love-struck teenager in the high school cafeteria. Now visualize yourself as a ten year-old child at the local county agricultural fair with your parents and siblings. As a family, you go into the main entertainment venue at the fair and sit in the front row, waiting with barely controlled excitement for the world-renowned hypnotist (self-proclaimed) to take the stage. With your family, you watch in amazement and amusement as the hypnotist puts an older man into a trance and has him waddling around the stage, quacking like a duck. For the next week, you keep swinging pocket watches in front of your brother, trying to hypnotize him, but you aren't successful. For years after, you think about that day, wondering why you couldn't make your brother do stupid and embarrassing things. It has to be a faked performance, right?

Is hypnosis real? Yes, it is very real, and you can learn to hypnotize yourself and others.

History of Hypnosis

Now that you have learned the basics of the ideas behind hypnosis, let's get into more specific information. What is the history of hypnosis, and how has it changed over the years? Is it only for entertainment purposes? What are the behavioral implications for it? Who can practice it and how? What are the ethical ramifications of using it?

The first recorded mentions of what would later be known as hypnotism come from the mid to late 1700s, when a healer named Franz Mesmer started his own practice of using magnets on the human body and inducing a state of altered consciousness in his clients (Hunter, 2010). He referred to this as animal magnetism. Toward the end of his career, Mesmer began to believe that the altered state was due to his own behaviors, such as the tone of his voice, and not his magnets. Later, a surgeon named Baird officially coined the term hypnosis, referring to a sleep-like state after the Greek god of sleep, Hypnos.

As Baird's work in the field of hypnosis continued, specifically looking at its use with regards to health and behavior, others took the idea and transformed it into a spiritual and potentially religious one. Inducing such states became part of the religious rituals of some groups in that time period, and continues in some fundamentalist religions to this day. While most current religions do recognize the positive uses of hypnosis to help with stress, health and negative behavioral patterns, there are some that continue to use hypnosis as a tool to convince parishioners and/or believers to donate money or other properties to their congregations or leaders. The use of hypnosis has also been used in religious communities that believe that homosexuality is a sinful choice as part of their treatment to supposedly change the person's sexuality. In and of itself, hypnosis is not a religious act; nor is it an act that is intended or believed to connect to a higher divine power of some sort.

As noted earlier, hypnosis has been recognized for centuries.

After the work of Braid, other scientists developed the idea of hypnosis causing ideomotor responses. Ideomotor refers to the brain or ideas (ideo) and the body's muscular responses (motor). Basically, the theory stated that putting ideas into someone's brain would lead to them being able to physically respond to suggestions. For example, planting the idea that when you hear a specific word, you need to kick out physically is an example of the ideomotor use of hypnosis. When hypnosis was used this way, patients were often induced into physical movement, such as walking, dancing or jumping, showing the brain and motor connection.

Later on, many researchers, including Freud, integrated hypnosis into their practices. The ideomotor theory of hypnosis carried on for many years, in which the hypnotist gave suggestions to the mind of the client, and their bodies responded to the commands — hence the prevalence of hypnotists at fairs making strangers quack like a duck. Even at the time of the primarily ideomotor view of hypnosis, psychologists began to ponder the use of hypnosis in terms of behavior, rather than just motor responses.

In the 1920s and 30s, hypnosis in a mental health therapeutic setting as we know it now began to develop, largely due to the work of psychologists and researchers Clark Hull and Milton Erickson. Erickson continued to work on refining the practice up until his death in 1980. In his work, Erickson stressed the importance of the unconscious mind and how clinical therapeutic suggestions could impact human behavior. Erickson also stressed the importance of non-verbal communication in humans. Hull and Erickson promoted the idea that hypnosis could be used to tap into our inner thought process and motivation, and open the mind to suggestions of ways to improve physical and mental health (Hunter, 2010).

Currently, hypnosis is usually seen in three arenas: the entertainment world, medicine and psychotherapy. All use it in different ways, some to entertain; some to heal or change a physical reality; some to lessen stress and improve mental health. For example, it may be used in a Las Vegas show to convince a spectator that they are no longer afraid of snakes, and therefore can hold a boa constrictor. It may be used to lower blood pressure through reduction of a person's stress responses. It may be used in therapy to identify emotional triggers and lessen the reaction to those events or situations. Hypnosis can also be used in other arenas, which we will discuss in a later chapter.

Myths About Hypnosis

The most common myth about hypnosis is that the hypnotized person loses complete control of their mind and body while in the hypnotic trance or state. That is not the case. The person is more open to the suggestions of others and changing their own behavior but has not lost control of their body.

Another myth is that the state can be so strong that it can be triggered in other places and at other times by trigger words or movements. While there have been a few cases reported — specifically in research trials about the use of hypnosis in the intelligence/military world — in which subjects have responded to the suggestions made under hypnosis much later, that is rare, and has only occurred in studies where it was the intended outcome (Navarro, 2015).

Another myth is that people can be hypnotized without their knowledge. Covert hypnosis is a reality, but it is likely that the subject of covert hypnosis knows at least that someone is trying to deeply connect with them and may be trying to influence their thought patterns.

A final myth? That in order to be hypnotized, you need to stare at a rhythmically moving object, such as the iconic watch on a chain, a metronome, or a finger swinging back and forth. The truth is that some hypnotists do use an object on which the subject focuses while being led into the suggestible state, but they may also just use their voices or a fixed object on which the subject focuses.

How Hypnosis Can Be Used

Being hypnotized means that you are in a trance-like or exceedingly relaxed and focused state of mind, in which your mind is open (and potentially vulnerable) to suggestions. The body tends to be very relaxed, and often the blood pressure lowers during a hypnotic event. The state is induced by someone trained as a hypnotist or hypnotherapist, using repetition of verbal comments and specific visual imagery.

Hypnotists are those that use hypnosis in entertainment as part of the mentalist arts referenced earlier, or people who use them in their daily personal or work lives, but not as part of a medical or mental health practice. Hypnotherapists, however, use hypnosis in medical or mental health/behavioral treatments. In order to be a hypnotherapist, the practitioner must be trained by a reputable program, may be required to be licensed (depending on where they are working), and is usually monitored or supervised in some way.

People who are hypnotized may or may not remember what happens while they are in that trance-like state, but consistently report feeling safe and relaxed while in the trance. Again, people do not lose control of the body or really even of the mind while hypnotized; they are only more open to suggestions regarding their behavior, health or past events.

In the medical world, hypnosis is used to control pain and some other medical issues and to control anxiety about medical procedures. Some common medical issues treated through hypnosis include pain management, blood pressure, hot flashes because of menopause, and side effects of treatments such as nausea caused by chemotherapy.

From a clinical therapeutic sense, hypnosis is used to change or control undesirable behaviors and also to allow people to address traumatic past issues. For example, it has been used to treat adults who were sexually abused as children, helping them to process and heal from that abuse. It also commonly addresses behavior such as smoking, overeating, chewing fingernails, the urge to self-harm, bedwetting, nightmares or night terrors, anxiety, and depression. The use of hypnosis for such a purpose is usually done in conjunction with other treatment modalities, such as medication or nutritional support.

During the 1980s, there was a heavy use of hypnosis to recover repressed memories in children and adults regarding abuse. During this time period, the subjects were hypnotized and then asked questions regarding potential past abuse. There were many high profile cases across the United States and Canada in which children and adults accused childcare providers, educators and pastors of ritualized sexual abuse after having been treated for repressed memories through hypnosis (Hunter, 2010).

Now, the work on the supposed retrieval of repressed memories is controversial and largely debunked, as it was found that several very high profile practitioners were planting seeds of memories while the child or adult was in a vulnerable and suggestible state. Later, criminal investigations found that many of these supposedly repressed memories were false and planted, and they overturned convictions, and ultimately convicted the hypnotherapists for their roles in these cases. There have also been cases where hypnotherapists were later revealed to have sexually assaulted their clients while hypnotized, leading to careful regulation of licensure of hypnotherapists (Hunter, 2010).

There also have been cases where hypnotherapists planted ideas regarding phobias or negative behaviors in order to then treat the subject for them. Again, this diminished the respectability of hypnosis as a treatment modality for a very long time.

Considering that hypnosis involves inducing a trance-like state in which the client or patient is very susceptible to suggestion, is it safe? What are the drawbacks? Overall, hypnotism is very safe as long as the hypnotist and hypnotherapist are well-trained and set controls in place for the safety of the client. For example, if someone is being hypnotized in an entertainment setting, the control words or movements need to be limited to only the hypnotist using them, to ensure that someone is not triggered into the state of hypnosis in uncontrolled situations. In the medical or therapeutic world, it again needs to be controlled and carefully monitored.

Side effects associated with hypnosis, although rare, can occur. Headaches, increased anxiety, false memories, confusion, dizziness and drowsiness can all occur. It is important to have someone with you to drive you home after being hypnotized, as you may be confused or disoriented.

How to Hypnotize Yourself and Others

So, you have decided to get hypnotized for medical or mental health (behavioral) reasons. Now what?

First, we will look at being hypnotized yourself by a hypnotist or hypnotherapist. Start by researching your options of practitioners. Ask a lot of questions. Are they licensed in your state or province to practice hypnosis? For how long have they been licensed? Have there been any judgments against them for malpractice? What is their background in terms of medical training and mental health work? How have they used hypnosis in treatments before? Have they ever treated exactly what you want to address before? If they haven't, look elsewhere for a hypnotherapist. Where did they train and for how long? How long have they been practicing hypnotherapy? What are their thoughts on repressed memories, and will they be attempting to have you look back at past experiences? If so, make sure the appointment is being audio or video taped and that you will have access to the recording if you wish so that you can know what was suggested to you about your past. What safeguards are in place to make sure the process will be safe and appropriate? Fees? Insurance? Follow-up appointments? Collaboration with your other practitioners? For example, if you are going into hypnotherapy to control your high blood pressure, you want the hypnotherapist to collaborate with your primary care physician so that your blood pressure doesn't drop too suddenly without medical supervision.

Insist on getting references — and not just written ones. Any practitioner that balks at providing names of clients with whom you can speak (with their permission) is not someone you want to put you into a vulnerable and suggestible state.

Once you are confident in the training and respectability of the practitioner, you need to get ready for the first session. Have someone ready to drive you home. Wear comfortable clothes and shoes. Be well-hydrated and rested. Be open to the idea of the treatment.

In the therapeutic setting, your practitioner will explain what will happen during the appointment and ask you if you have any questions prior to starting treatment. The person will review the goals of your treatment plan to make sure that you are both aligned in your understanding of the goals and how you plan to achieve them. Then they will start talking to you in a very relaxed and calming tone, looking to increase your sense of safety and relaxation. While you are in the suggestible state, the therapist will suggest ways in which you can control your behavior or ways in which you can respond to situations. For example, it may be suggested that every time you would previously have had the urge to eat a chocolate donut, instead, you will now crave a piece of fruit such as an apple. Or it may be suggesting to you that you want to chew gum instead of smoking a cigarette. If behavioral change is the goal of hypnosis, the hypnotherapist will usually plant vivid and positive mental images of you achieving your goals.

At the end of the session, the hypnotherapist will bring you out of the state, or will have set it up so that you can bring yourself out. At this point, when you return to your normal state of consciousness, you are likely to still be very relaxed. Very often, in this form of hypnosis, you will have some memory of what happened while you were hypnotized.

Over time, you may be able to self-induce a hypnotic state and be able to self-hypnotize. This is often taught to those suffering from severe phobias or anxiety so that they can induce that state of calm in situations that would otherwise trigger them.

Does hypnosis work? Is it worth the hype it has received? Yes, hypnosis works in specific situations, especially if the subject truly believes it will. It has been found to be very effective for behavioral changes such as weight loss and smoking cessation. It has also been found effective in dealing with anxiety around medical procedures or treatments.

Can anyone be hypnotized? No. Most people can be hypnotized, but for some, it is very difficult to induce the suggestible state in them. Overall, the quicker someone can be induced into that state, the more likely it is that the behavior modification will work. For example, if you can enter the hypnotic state quickly, it is more likely that you will be successful in using it to stop smoking.

Now that you know the history and widely accepted uses of hypnosis, can you learn to hypnotize others and yourself? Absolutely, although you need to be cognizant of the potential risks of trying to hypnotize others. There are two ways to hypnotize others: openly and covertly.

To openly hypnotize someone, you need to start by getting a willing participant. Find someone who wants to try the process with you, making sure that they do not have a history of mental illness or abuse, as you may trigger responses in them that are unwanted or unplanned.

Both of you should move into a quiet, distraction-free and comfortable space. Remove distractions such as cell phones or televisions, and look for ways to limit extraneous noises that could distract the two of you. Have your partner sit or lie down comfortably. Make sure that you won't be interrupted. Explain that at no time will they lose control of their body or mind and that they will only be in a very relaxed state with increased focus and clarity. Clarify what they would like to work on through being hypnotized, such as feeling more relaxed about an upcoming family event. Double-check if the person has ever been hypnotized before. If they have, they are more likely to enter the trance-like state easily and quickly.

Start speaking to the person in a consistently calm and relaxing tone of voice. Use calming statements such as, "You are going to feel more and more relaxed, feeling your body sink into the chair as you sit back." Or, "As you relax, you will remain in complete control of yourself and will only do what feels right to you."

Then ask the person to focus on taking deep, regular breaths. Model for them what you want them to do with their breathing so that they can follow your pattern. Talk them through the breathing: "You are going to take a deep breath in through your nose when I do… Now breathe out through your mouth." Repeat this, focusing on deep breathing and getting oxygen into their system. The focus on breathing, just as in meditation, allows the subject to focus on something other than the actual hypnosis, and therefore may help them relax more quickly and move into the trance more readily.

Once the breathing pattern is established and rhythmic, ask the subject to focus their eyes on a fixed point of reference. Many hypnotherapists suggest their subjects focus on a spot right under one of the therapist's eyes or on a fixed object in the room. Remind the subject that closing their eyes is fine, or their eyes may remain open. If you see your subject's eyes wandering or moving around, gently remind them to focus back on one point, and if needed, pick a point for them, and keep quietly and gently reminding them to focus on that point.

Following a body relaxation pattern as used in meditation, guide your subject through feeling each part of their body and focusing on relaxing each part, starting with the toes and slowly moving up to the head. If they seem resistant to the process, instead switch to asking them to clench each part of the body and then relax it, such as curling up their toes before relaxing them fully, feeling them sink into the floor or the couch. Guide them into full relaxation, commenting in your calm and quiet voice about how relaxed they are getting and how safe and warm they feel. Comments such as, "As you listen to my voice, you are getting more and more relaxed and feeling safer and safer. The feeling is getting stronger, and you are fully relaxed," will help them focus and let them fall into the hypnotic state.

Then you are going to guide the subject down a figurative staircase with verbal directions, telling them they are walking down the stairs, going deeper and deeper into their own mind, and as they go down each step, they get more and more relaxed. Some hypnotherapists then use the imagery of a door at the bottom of the stairs, telling the subject that once they reach the door and open it, they will be in the fully relaxed state, safe and free of all worries, anxiety or pain.

Now, if you are doing this for more than just entertainment purposes, this is the point in which you can help others. For many subjects, just reaching that point of relaxation will lessen overall anxiety and help them feel more relaxed. For others, if they are struggling with a particular problem or issue, this relaxed state allows them to be guided to think of possible solutions or paths of action. For example, if someone hates their job but feels trapped with no options, hypnosis can help them to envision options or paths to follow in order to resolve or improve the situation. Even if you are not a professionally trained hypnotherapist, you can guide your subject into healthier life choices at this point, encouraging them to envision a life without smoking or with healthy food choices or other positive changes.

Then it is time to bring the subject out of the trance. You are again going to guide them with your words, bringing them back from the deeply relaxed state with comments such as, "I am going to count backwards from 20 (or any other number) and when I get to one, you will be fully awake and full of energy, ready for the rest of your day." Then, slowly and gently, count back to that number.

Once the subject is fully awake again, ask if they would be willing to talk about what they just experienced. Process how they felt during the session with them, and discuss how they feel now. Ask for suggestions. Thank them for joining you on this journey of trust.

Step by step, here is how you openly hypnotize someone:

- Step one: Determine who you want to hypnotize, and determine why you want to do it. Make sure the person is not mentally ill and does not have a history of trauma. Ask them if they would like to be hypnotized, and honor their feelings if they refuse or are hesitant.

- Step two: Both of you move to a quiet, distraction-free environment.

- Step three: Have the subject sit or lie down comfortably.

- Step four: Review the process and clarify goals.

- Step five: Start speaking to the person in a consistently calm and relaxing tone of voice.

- Step six: Instruct the subject to focus on taking deep regular breaths, and model the breathing pattern for them. Breathe in through the nose, filling the lungs, hold it, and breathe out through the mouth.

- Step seven: Instruct the subject to focus their eyes

on a fixed point. This may be a point on your face or a point in the room. Some hypnotherapists use a moving object, but that is not necessary and is unduly complicated for hypnosis outside of a formal health or mental health treatment plan.

• Step eight: Guide the subject through a systematic pattern of body relaxation, moving from the toes to the top of the head. Have them focus carefully on each part of the body, encouraging them to relax, feeling like they are sinking into the chair or couch.

• Step nine: Guide the subject down a figurative staircase with verbal directions.

• Step ten: Work on the goals established prior to the session.

• Step eleven: Bring the subject out of the hypnotic state.

• Step twelve: Discuss and reflect on the process, and thank them for working with you.

• Follow-up: Determine if you want to continue to use hypnosis together.

But is this the only way to hypnotize someone, asking them for their permission? No, of course not. There also is covert hypnotism, in which the subject does not know they are being hypnotized.

For covert hypnotism, you need to be able to get the subject's brain to focus elsewhere, so you can get inside their thought patterns and manipulate their behavior or responses. The easiest way to do this is to engage the brain by putting forward unfinished business. The brain automatically compartmentalizes things that have been completed or done, such as when we complete an action like putting away the clean clothes after doing the laundry. By instead introducing unfinished business, the brain gets obsessed by trying to figure out what needs to happen so that the subject becomes more susceptible to suggestion. In the most basic terms, the unfinished business will engage the thinking parts of the brain and keep them busy, allowing the hypnotist or hypnotherapist to access the rest of the brain easily.

Try telling them a story without an ending — leave them hanging. Make ambiguous statements. Interrupt normal patterns, or ask them to imagine something. Any of those techniques will keep them from focusing on your immediate behavior and instead leave them open to subconscious suggestions. Just remember to use this ability and skill well and with integrity.

Want to hypnotize someone without their knowledge or agreement? The steps are:

- Step one: As with open hypnosis, determine who you want to hypnotize, and determine why you want to do it. Make sure the person is not mentally ill and does not have a history of trauma. If you are unsure of the person's stability or history, err on the side of caution, and pick another subject.

- Step two: Both of you move to a quiet, distraction-free environment. While it may be difficult to do this when the subject doesn't know they are going to be hypnotized, still strive for a spot that doesn't have electronics to distract, limit extraneous noise, soften the lighting, and pick a spot with comfortable seating.

- Step three: Have the subject sit comfortably.

- Step four: Start speaking to the person in a consistently calm and relaxing tone of voice.

- Step five: Model deep breathing without mentioning that you're doing it. The subject is likely to align their breathing with yours without realizing it. Again, breathe in deeply, preferably through your nose, hold it, and release it out through your mouth. If that seems odd in the situation, breathe in and out as normal, but more slowly and very rhythmically.

- Step six: Use open-ended questions to open the subject's brain to your suggestions.

- Step seven: Work on the goals you established through gentle suggestions.

- Step eight: Bring the subject out of the hypnotic state slowly and gently, using positive wording to help them feel safe and supported.

- Step nine: Process and reflect on the hypnosis when the subject leaves the room.

- Step ten (long-term): Continue the process regularly until the goal is achieved.

Now that you know how to hypnotize others openly or covertly, how do you self-hypnotize? You follow many of the same steps of simple breathing meditation.

Find a warm, safe spot that is free of distractions. Get comfortable. Focus on your breathing pattern, counting your breathing repetitions. Start at your toes, and consciously work on relaxing each part of your body, one by one. When you reach the point of full relaxation, allow your brain to visualize healthy responses or positive changes you want to make in your life. Then welcome yourself back into the world, holding onto that deep feeling of peace and safety.

To self-hypnotize:

- Preparation: Decide why you want to self-hypnotize. Do you have a specific career or personal goal, or is it more for relaxation and stress reduction? Is it to increase or free your creativity? Lower your blood pressure? Calm yourself in preparation of family time during the holidays? Prepare yourself mentally for a job interview? What is your goal, and why is this goal important to you? Clearly articulate your goals for self-hypnosis.

- Step one: Move to a quiet, distraction-free environment, preferably with soft lighting or natural light.

- Step two: Sit or lie down comfortably.

- Step three: Focus on taking deep regular breaths in through the nose and out through the mouth, holding them in between. Feel your lungs expanding and contracting, and notice how the air feels going in and coming out.

- Step four: Follow a systematic pattern of body relaxation, moving from the toes to the top of the head. Make sure that every part of your body is fully relaxed and feels heavy and soft.

- Step five: Focus on your personal goal, and think of ways in which you can work on that goal.

- Step six: Bring yourself back to the present slowly.

- Follow-up: Practice self-hypnosis often in order to achieve your goals.

Hypnosis, either of oneself or of others, can be very successful for bringing about behavioral changes or in reducing anxiety and phobias. In most cases however, formal hypnotherapy should be combined with other counseling or support in order to achieve the greatest positive growth.

Chapter 5: Deception and Neuro-Linguistic Programming

Now we are ready to learn more deeply about deception and neuro-linguistic programming.

Starting with deception, visualize yourself as a junior in high school, ready to start looking into colleges and universities. You have been an outstanding student, both academically and civically. Therefore, you are surprised when your school college counselor calls you in, saying that your college applications aren't going to be interesting enough and you haven't "done" enough to get their attention. In a flurry of activity, you then sign up to another sport, start volunteering more, and make sure your grades are even better. Later on, after you have been accepted to every college you applied to, she tells you that she had knowingly deceived you about your prospects as a way to motivate you further. Deception was used to change your behavior. Are you angry because of the deception or thrilled because of the outcome?

In order to visualize how neuro-linguistic programming could be used in your life, think about youth sports. Young athletes are told to watch professional athletes perform; they read about the athletes; they emulate and copy their practice routines. In a very simple form, those young athletes are following the mental maps of the pros and superimposing them over their own inner maps to set their goals and achieve them.

Now that you have a mental image of the use of both deception and neuro-linguistic programming, let's delve deeper into both topics.

Neuro-linguistic programming takes the understanding of verbal and non-verbal communication stressed by mind-reading, combines it with the deeply relaxed and focused state of hypnosis, and adds to it the idea of a personal inner map of your beliefs and goals. It helps you to take your own mental map and superimpose it over the map of someone you admire, and follow the steps they did to hopefully achieve the same outcome.

For example, if you want to be a newspaper journalist, learning about the mental map of the greatest reporters and how they achieved their success will allow you to understand how to follow in their footsteps. Covert NLP is using the same ideas but working without the subject's knowledge or permission. Covert NLP is also often referred to as conversational hypnosis, as it relies on getting past someone's defenses to their true thoughts, feelings and goals.

To practice NLP covertly, use the steps for mind-reading after clearly understanding both your own goals and the inner mental map of the subject. Then use the steps of hypnosis to start planting the suggestions that will merge your goals into the maps of others.

Overview of Deception and Neuro-Linguistic Programming

You are now well-versed in mind-reading theory and practice, and hypnosis both of others and yourself. Now it is time to move on to deception and neuro-linguistic programming. While a brief overview of them was given earlier in the book, now we will dig more deeply into the practices.

What is deception in psychological terms, and how is it used? Deception in psychology is the same idea as deception in any other arena. It is speaking and acting in an untruthful manner with or about your subject for a particular purpose.

The most common example of formal deception in a professional setting is the use of placebos in medicine and medical trials. In such a situation, a patient goes in complaining of an ailment, and the doctor feels that it is most likely a psychosomatic or false complaint. As the patient is so insistent on the existence of the illness, the doctor prescribes a sugar pill or placebo as part of the treatment. Interestingly, many patients have shown true improvement with placebos because they believe they are receiving the real medication as treatment.

Taking it a step further, many formal medical and psychiatric clinical trials also use placebos as part of the process. A placebo is a pill given to treat an illness that does not actually have medicine in it. It is fake medication. Some patients receive the real medication and others receive a placebo, and the responses to both are measured. All such clinical trials list the side effects and effectiveness of the medications, both for the placebos and the real medication. Often, the group that received the placebo will show many of the same reactions, improvements or side effects as those receiving the real medication, as their belief in what should or will happen is so strong. The power of suggestibility is amazing!

In psychology, deception is used to see how subjects will respond in a given situation, and it is based on the idea that if subjects understand the full truth of the study or experiment, they will respond in the way that they feel is socially acceptable or in the way they feel the researcher wants them to respond. For example, studies on children often show that children will respond in the way they feel the adult researchers want them to respond, even if it is not the way they truly feel.

By the mid-1950s, deception was being used more widely in psychological research. In 1954, psychologist and researcher W. Edgar Vinacke started publically raising his concerns about deception in research studies. At the time, Vinacke's fears fell on deaf ears, as the field was becoming more enamored of such studies and combining scientific research methods into the field of psychology (Mann, 2016).

The most famous psychological experiment on deception occurred in 1963. In that study, Yale University professor and researcher Stanley Milgram ran an obedience study. In the study, the participants were not told of the true research question. The study focused on a classroom situation, in which one subject was in the role of the instructor, and another was in the role of a student. When the student answered questions incorrectly, the instructor administered what they thought was an electrical shock as punishment. The true purpose of the study was to see if the instructor would eventually stop shocking the student, even if the answers were incorrect, due to the student complaining of pain. Milgram was looking to see if the subjects in the role of instructor would continue to obey the instruction to shock the student for incorrect answers, even if they knew they were causing increasing pain to the student. At the end of the study, Milgram proved that 65 percent of the subjects who had the role of instructor continued to administer shocks, even as they knew they were causing pain (Mann, 2016).

After the experiment concluded, Milgram informed all participants of the true basis of the experiment. Many of the participants recognized that he needed to deceive them to get a true sense of what they would do in terms of obedience of an order. Others were horrified and angry at the deception, leading to formal complaints that led to changes in some guiding principles and procedures for psychological testing. Many other psychological researchers also decried Milgram's study, accusing him of both deceiving his subjects and gratuitously causing pain. Those colleagues felt that both his deception and inducing pain were psychologically harmful to his subjects and were therefore unethical.

In the years since Milgram's study, the use of deception is much more carefully regulated in research studies. While it still is used in pharmaceutical trials, participants are told they may or may not receive the real medication. Deception is still used in other research studies, especially in terms of giving misleading information in a study in order to connect with a subject's core values and beliefs. However, this use of deception continues to be controversial. The American Psychological Association does allow deception to be used in research studies, as long as the deception is not likely to cause pain, suffering or psychological harm (Mann, 2016).

Outside of psychological research, how is deception used? It continues to be used widely in interrogations, such as in giving misleading information to a suspect to get information out of them or so that they think someone has given information about them. For example, when police know that someone has committed a murder but have not found the body, deceptive and misleading comments about other people giving information may motivate the suspect to give up the location of the body because they think the police already know where it is. Deception by police interrogators has also caused many innocent people to be convicted, as they confessed to crimes they didn't commit because they were led to believe that there was evidence of a crime. Deception is also used by the police in telling suspects that if they confess to the crime, the punishment will be less than if they don't confess.

Deception is also used in many workplace environments, both formally and informally, by employers and employees. Formal deception by employers continues to be a controversial practice. In this form of workplace deception, misleading information is shared with employees to give them a false reality to bring about specific behavioral responses. For example, telling employees that sales are down toward the end of a quarter to motivate them to sell even more, is a formal deception by an employer. Another example is a supervisor telling an employee that their upcoming evaluation will show they need to work harder to motivate the employee to work even more diligently.

Deception in the workplace also occurs between employees and may be both planned and subconscious. For example, an employee may make misleading statements about a colleague to improve his or her own social standing in the office. An employee may withhold information so that a colleague is unprepared for a situation. Both of those formal and planned deceptions mean that a colleague looks bad in the eyes of others, and the deceiver is likely to look better. It may also be subconscious, such as in the case of an employee who's terrified of interpersonal conflict not telling a colleague when they have made a mistake, and instead telling a little white lie about everything being just fine.

How else is deception used in professional settings? Many retailers use scarcity marketing as a tool, telling their customers that they were almost out or had sold out of a product in order to boost their overall sales.

To use deception in either your personal or professional life, follow these steps:

- Step one: Determine the goal of your deception and who you plan to deceive, and come up with a plan of how to either withhold information or share incorrect or misleading information.

● Step two: Follow your outlined plan, keeping it as simple as possible.

● Step three: Make sure to keep the truth and the deception clear in your own mind so as to not cause confusion or make mistakes.

● Step four: Use the resulting behaviors of the person or persons deceived to move toward your goal.

● Step five: Determine the follow-up steps needed to achieve your goal or goals.

So, now that we know about deception, what is neuro-linguistic programming? As noted before, it is a psychological viewpoint that says that by analyzing the behaviors and strategies of the highly successful people we emulate, we can use those same strategies to reach our own personal goals. It is a belief system that says that our language, thoughts and behaviors are all connected and lead to outcomes, and by using the knowledge well, the outcomes can be what we (or others) want them to be.

In NLP, the theory states that any action of a human is positive, but it may not have the desired outcome. Even in that situation, however, the person can learn from the situation and use that information to move toward goals.

Where did NLP develop? The epicenter of the birth of this movement was in the 1970s in Santa Cruz, California. There, at the University of California, researchers John Grinder and Richard Bandler, neither of whom were psychologists, developed their theory, connecting it back to much of the work of Milton Erickson. Grinder and Bandler promoted the idea that excellent communicators have shared patterns of communication, and that it is possible to identify linguistic patterns that show the inner workings of the thought process. As the popularity of the theory grew, Grinder and Bandler emphasized that they could use their theory outside of psychology, specifically recommending using it in business, professional sports, military, marketing, education, law, and other professional fields (Mann, 2016).

How does it work? The theory states that an effective communicator can explain how they have achieved success or completed a specific task. Sharing that information with others clearly means that the recipient of the information can understand and visualize what happened and then can follow the same model to achieve the same outcome, or follow the same model to achieve their own personal goal or goals. Those who practice NLP believe that by clear communication and by following the model, others can bring about the change they want to see in their lives (Navarro, 2015).

NLP stresses learning, communication and change. Practitioners believe that each person has their own highly developed inner map of what they believe is their own reality. They also believe that each map is unique and that no person has an inner map that aligns with those of others or fully with reality. By practicing NLP, people get to understand the inner maps of themselves and others and overlay those maps for specific reasons, creating a new map that is more multidimensional and more accurate about reality.

In NLP, there is also a clear belief in the mind-body connection. Practitioners believe in the idea of physically replicating the actions of those they emulate in order to make the body and mind come into alignment. For example, a youth wanting to achieve world fame in free rock climbing (without ropes and harnesses) would not only study the written and verbal accounts of great free climbers; they would also attempt to follow their climbing routes exactly in order to connect the learning communicated with the physical body.

Modeling, action and effective communication are key elements of neuro-linguistic programming. The belief is that if an individual can understand how another person accomplishes a task, the process may be copied and communicated to others so that they too can accomplish it.

In NLP, practitioners believe that every person develops their own inner personal mental map. The map is formed by all of the input from our senses, our experiences and our backgrounds. It is unique to each person, and often when understood by other people, seems to be slightly skewed or removed from true reality. They believe that if a person can explain their own inner map and how they achieved their success, they will be able to share this information with others so they can follow the same steps.

These personal maps develop over the course of our lifetime, and the information comes from all of our senses. The maps develop as humans take in sounds, sensations, tastes, smells, movements and communication from others. Those sources of input combine into a unique primary representational system (PRS), which truly is the inner map. As an NLP practitioner works with a client, the practitioner has to understand their inner map and PRS, and work to align their own map with the client's. NLP practitioners work on gaining access to the PRS of clients through reading non-verbal cues such as eye movement and body language.

Once the practitioner has accessed the PRS and understands the thought process, behavior, goals and emotions of the client, the practitioner then works with them to identify and build on their positive skills and attributes, and helps them identify those behaviors and attributes that are working against their progress. The practitioner then works with the client to identity positive changes to replace the negative aspects that are holding them back from achieving their goals.

Believers stress that NLP can quickly bring about changes in behavior and help people achieve their personal and professional goals. They stress that it combines the mind-body work with outstanding interpersonal communication and helps to improve creativity as clients learn to think about the thinking of others.

Currently, NLP therapists use this model to treat anxiety disorders, depression, addiction, issues with attention and focus, obsessive-compulsive disorder, and other psychiatric and mental health issues. With some of these disorders, NLP therapy is combined with other treatment modalities such as medication. While NLP therapists claim that their process is widely and consistently successful in treating such mental health disorders, there is no consistent empirical data to support those claims yet. Interestingly, Bandler himself has said that this is not a field that should be empirically tested; instead, practitioners should use it in a less formal and restrictive manner.

How is the field of NLP changing and evolving? Some educational researchers have suggested that students with special needs (supported through special education services) would benefit from the communication skills and visualization that NLP encourages. While some schools have used some pieces of NLP, it is just in the early research phases and not in full implementation consistently, and there is no empirical data to date on the effectiveness of the practice in schools.

One of the most interesting components of NLP connects back to deception. Practitioners claim that changes in eye movement show dishonest behavior, including lying. They stress that being trained in NLP helps in the detection of deceptive behaviors. However, in studies conducted using NLP practitioners and non-practitioners, there was no statistical evidence to show that the NLP therapists were more likely to recognize deception by seeing eye movement than the non-NLP therapists were (Navarro, 2015). The data from these studies cast some doubt on the effectiveness of using NLP as a tool, although many practitioners and former clients swear that it has helped them to achieve their personal and professional goals.

How Do You Practice Deception and NLP?

Practicing deception is frightfully easy. In order to do so, you need to make a decision to knowingly lie or mislead others, or omit information so that the other person does not have all of the information — or accurate information — they need to assess the situation correctly. You start by sharing only enough information to bring about the change you desire.

For example, in a really small example of deception bringing about a desired outcome, think of when your secretary calls and says that she is running late because she is stopping for coffee. You tell her not to worry about being late — after all, you are starting the day slowly because you didn't have time for coffee and breakfast because you were too busy. This is a complete lie — you had your normal cup of coffee and a bowl of yogurt, but you really want a chocolate donut and a cappuccino. Because of your lie, she jumps to offer to pick you up a coffee, and wouldn't a chocolate donut make you feel better? You hang up, smiling broadly, as you just lied your way into a great treat.

What about NLP? Can anyone practice the NLP model? Currently, there is not a clear training model or licensing model for NLP therapists, leading to many self-taught therapists who claim expertise. If you are seeking NLP to address your own needs or the needs of a loved one, make sure to seek someone who has extensive training, shares references, and has past experience of using NLP to address whatever issue you are seeking to address.

Do you want to practice NLP? If so, the best way is to start by reading one of the myriad of books on the subject, and watch videos about NLP. There are many outstanding and clear short videos on NLP on the Internet, and they can help explain the process and its steps by modeling them in the video. The videos and books also have links to training programs or respected practitioners.

To practice covert neuro-linguistic programming:

- Step one: Be mindful of your own body and emotions.

- Step two: Understand your own inner mental map, including your own goals, and how you plan to reach those goals.

- Step three: Pick your subject for the process.

- Step four: Determine how that subject can help you achieve your goals or the goals you have for that person.

- Step five: Invite the person to a distraction-free environment like you did in the covert hypnosis discussed earlier.

- Step six: Use your mind-reading and hypnosis skills to understand your subject's motivations and emotions and also get them into a suggestible state of mind.

- Step seven: Start planting suggestions of how they can change their behavior in such a way as to help you achieve the goals you have set.

- Step eight (long-term): Continue to repeat the process, guiding the subject along the clear steps to achieve the goals.

If you want to start practicing some of the techniques of NLP for yourself now, start in the same way you did for self-hypnosis. Get comfortable and seated. Take in a deep breath through your nose, filling your lungs, and hold it. Breathe out through your mouth. Repeat this several times. Then systematically focus on relaxing each part of your body from your toes to your head. Feel the heaviness of your body in the chair; feel how your body is in contact with the chair. Close your eyes, and visualize a warm, sunny day. Feel the warmth of the sun on your face, and let yourself just relax and enjoy the feeling. Ask your mind to further the visualization by adding in sounds such as ocean waves, or feelings and experiences like visualizing eating a perfect strawberry. When you are done with your visualization, open your eyes, and let yourself reflect on what you experienced during the process. Are you more relaxed now? Are you more energized, at peace, ready to focus again?

Pros and Cons

So, how would you connect and use deception and neuro-linguistic programming in your professional life, especially if you are in a leadership or supervisory role, and what are the pros and cons of using each? The pros of deception are simple: it can be a very effective motivational tool if all you are concerned with is a particular outcome. You want to increase sales? Deceiving your employees that sales are off and that they need to sell more in order to keep their jobs is likely to make them work as hard as they can to achieve higher sales numbers. However, if they find out that you deceived them, it is likely to be a very negative work environment.

NLP, however, allows for positive visualization and focused growth, based on clear communication, shared understanding, and a clear visual map of how to achieve the goal. While many of the positive pieces of NLP can be self-taught through reading and online learning, in order to fully implement it in a workplace, there would need to be adequate training to the NLP practitioner and clear guidelines about when to use it and for what purpose.

Now that we have looked at NLP in general, we need to look at what is referred to as covert NLP. Covert, meaning in secret, neuro-linguistic programming is used as a way to motivate others around you without their knowledge. Covert NLP is also commonly referred to as conversational hypnosis.

Covert NLP embraces the idea of secretly moving around the conscious cognitive responses of another human being in order to directly plant ideas, thoughts and emotions into their subconscious for a specific purpose — for example, moving past the fiscal stinginess of a customer to engage their emotions so that they will buy more of your product, or getting a crowd ready for the launch of a new product by triggering a warm emotional response, regardless of the product or their preconceived perceptions about it. While many major corporations have publicly denied using such strategies, many use the same pre-launch promoters who have extensive training in covert NLP.

You many have already experienced covert NLP or conversational hypnosis without realizing it. For example, you may have sat through what should have been a regular, non-emotive meeting, and instead came out of the meeting emotionally charged about something that normally would not evoke strong emotions. Or you met a new colleague or supervisor, and immediately felt a strong emotional connection to them. Usually, that means that outside of your cognitive processing, you were impacted by covert NLP or conversational hypnosis.

Ethical Questions About Deception and NLP

Is it okay to deceive others in order to achieve a desired outcome? For example, when Congress was told that Iraq had weapons of mass destruction, it led to the United States invading Iraq. Later, the deception was uncovered, but the leader of Iraq had been ousted. Was that deception worth the outcome? If deceiving an employee about his or her performance review motivates them to work harder, is it worth it for the company's bottom line? Is lying to a medical patient in a trial about the medication or placebo they are taking justified by the knowledge gained in the trial?

The gains in knowledge or performance may be beneficial in many ways. In NLP, the understanding of a person's inner map helps the practitioner know how to focus them and motivate them toward goals. But what if the goals in question are not the personal goals of the subject but instead are the desired outcome of the company? What if there was an outstanding scientist who wanted to work on climate change? This scientist was hired by a company that was financially supported by the oil industry, and through using NLP, the company guided her to visualize their next research project. Instead of helping her achieve her own goals and follow her own beliefs, the company's NLP practitioner guided her to think about ways in which petrochemicals could be used more widely, regardless of the environmental impact.

What are the ethical dilemmas in covert NLP? Again, as with full deception, it is manipulating or motivating others without their knowledge for your personal or organizational goals. While the outcomes may not be negative or harmful, is manipulating others without their knowledge and permission ethical?

Both deception and neuro-linguistic programming can be used to motivate others and bring about behavioral change. It is up to both the practitioners and the subjects to make sure they are not being used or abused in the process.

Chapter 6: How Are These Techniques Used in Our Modern World

Now that you understand the basics of the theories of these techniques and have information about practicing them yourself, it is time to identify and understand how they are used in the world around us. Each day, some of these techniques sneak into our lives, whether or not we fully recognize them.

The strategies of mind-reading, hypnosis, deception and covert neuro-linguistic programming are interwoven through many aspects of our lives. Their use can be seen in the marketing of goods and services, in our military and intelligence communities, and in education, amongst other fields. Many times, the reasons for using them are positive, as are the outcomes, although at times, they may be used in what can be seen as nefarious ways. In all cases, there is a need to look at whether the desired or expected outcome is worth the potential pitfalls of the practice.

Marketing

It has happened to everyone. That moment when you realize that you absolutely have to buy or get a particular product. For the past week, the ad running on television has caught your eye and your full attention, and the soft music playing in the background of the ad makes you feel warm and happy. Now you are standing at the store, waiting to spend way more than you should on a product that you don't need because the ad campaign caught you emotionally. Cell phones are the perfect example of this phenomenon. Year-by-year now, there is very little difference in the smartphones on the market, but the marketing campaigns convince you that you can't survive without that newest version of the phone.

This is not by chance. Marketing of products and services openly and covertly uses the techniques of mind-reading, hypnosis, deception and neuro-linguistic programming to get and keep your attention and motivate your spending.

For example, many companies that manufacture luxury goods will hire researchers to use groups of consumers of similar but competing products, hypnotize them through conversational hypnosis (covert NLP), and get a much deeper understanding of what they like and don't like about the competitors' products in order to make their products more appealing. For example, going back to the topic of cell phones, manufacturers of high-end products, such as the top-of-the-line electronics, will mine for information about why someone bought one particular smartphone or tablet over another, then work on changing their own product to get a larger share of the market.

Deception also frequently comes into marketing. For example, advertising a product for sale at a great price but having huge hidden sales fees that aren't shown in legible print in the ad is a form of deception. Fear is also often used in deceptive marketing campaigns. You know the campaigns — the ones where you're told to buy or use a particular product or else there will be a bad outcome. For example, if you don't buy that expensive alarm system, your beloved spouse, children and pets will be robbed and killed. Fear motivates sales. Deceptive descriptions may also be used, such as advertising that a product looks, tastes or reacts exactly like a more expensive alternative, leading to sales of the new product.

In all of these situations, the marketing is based on extensive research of the buying patterns of particular demographic groups, then works on understanding motivation, timing, emotions and thought patterns. Marketing researchers use many of the skills and steps used in mind-reading, hypnosis, and NLP to be able to openly or covertly observe and understand people and then manipulate them based on their understanding in order to motivate them to purchase whatever is being sold. It is not a coincidence that graduate programs in marketing and sales have a large component of psychology in their classes.

Military and Intelligence Work

Within the military and intelligence communities, these skills and techniques are frequently used. They are used on those working for the communities, on their adversaries, and on local civilian communities in areas of military conflicts. Both military and intelligence use the skills inherent in mind-reading and hypnosis for self-awareness, relaxation, focus, and understanding of the motivation and possible behaviors of others.

How else are the skills used? The understanding of emotion, the connection between mind and body, and motivation are all used in interrogation, incarceration, and in misinformation campaigns. As noted earlier, the deceptions used to justify the United States invading Iraq or deceptions used in misinformation campaigns during the Cold War have been instrumental in determining foreign policy. Misinformation campaigns have also been used in other diplomatic missions. Frequently, governments drop deceptive propaganda into civilian areas in order to develop allegiances or support networks or to convince the population to oppose particular groups or efforts.

Recent disclosures on the work of the United States' Central Intelligence Agency (CIA) over the years has shown the use of deception and other mind-control techniques in interrogation and intelligence gathering (Navarro, 2015). We have learned of the use of hypnosis in both their own agents and in trying to manipulate the agents of other countries. Mind-control programs have been developed, using the power of suggestion while in a hypnotic state to develop better agents or soldiers, planting thoughts regarding desired behavior into their minds and making them better at their jobs. Disclosures have shown that disinformation campaigns have been used in multiple countries and situations. They have shown that governments have held captives, who have been psychologically manipulated and possibly tortured by being deceived about their situations, families or other loved ones. There have also been many disclosures or resources shared in the last few years about the use of such techniques in military conflicts such as the war in Syria, the Vietnam War and World War II.

How are these techniques used in a positive manner? Soldiers and intelligence agents learn about verbal and non-verbal communication in order to elicit information and make informed decisions. They also learn these techniques in order to be able to self-monitor stress and focus and to calm anxiety as needed. Many elite soldiers speak openly about how important the skill of self-hypnosis is to them in terms of focus and ability to self-regulate stress and emotions.

Education

In the field of education, deception is most often used in research trials. In classrooms, especially in elementary and secondary classrooms, the emergence of the research on mind-reading, hypnosis and neuro-linguistic programming has been used in classroom management, in motivation and focus, and in improving overall behavior and mental health of students. Supervisors/school administrators use the knowledge in order to better work with students, faculty and staff, as well as parents and families. In all of those situations, the skills are supposed to be used to improve the educational outcomes for students. Many schools are now stressing the need for adults to be trained to recognize non-verbal cues in order to better understand the population with which they work.

There are situations in which these techniques are used in a more unseemly fashion in education, primarily in elementary and pre-collegiate schools. They are used at times in behavioral responses, using deception and misinformation in order to solicit information from students. Most often, this is seen in behavioral issues such as bullying and vandalism, when school personnel pretend to have information about the situation when they don't in order to get confessions, much as is done at times in police, military or intelligence interrogations. Students may also be deceived about their academic or athletic performance in order to motivate them to work harder and achieve more.

How is education likely to use these techniques in the future? More and more schools are looking at the connection between adverse childhood experiences (trauma) and academic performance. Faculty and staff are being trained to recognize the non-verbal cues from children that show they are triggered. They are learning to use many of the same techniques used in mind-reading, hypnosis and neuro-linguistic programming to work with this population of students. The adults are being trained to understand motivation, goals, the anatomy and functions of the brain, and how emotions impact behavior and focus. Faculties are working collaboratively to share their knowledge of students and families in order to make sure their responses are aligned with the needs of the students, while also focusing on the overall goal of educational/academic progress.

Why Are These Strategies Used, and What Outcomes Are Seen from Using Skills and Techniques?

These strategies are used in the fields of marketing, the military and intelligence communities, and education in order to get desired outcomes. Marketing departments use them to learn about their consumers and sell more products or services. They are used to drive continued consumption of goods, even when the goods are not needed. Military and intelligence agencies use them to both help their members be as mentally healthy and aware as possible, and also to get information from and control over adversaries. In education, they are used to get information and control behaviors of both adults and students, and hopefully to allow students to be able to better access their learning in schools.

Many schools are now stressing the importance of mindfulness. Students and adults are being taught about being centered, calm minds and bodies, and are learning to identify their own emotional triggers and how to respond to them. The sooner this self-awareness begins, the healthier students statistically seem to be in terms of mental health needs. Self-awareness and self-regulation skills have both physical and mental health benefits, and schools are recognizing and celebrating that fact.

In all of them, the strategies are used to control behavior in some way. They may be used to control the behavior of others, such as in marketing, or of the self, such as soldiers self-hypnotizing.

With the knowledge of how often marketing and education alone use the techniques, it is clear that every person in Western society is impacted by the strategies on a daily basis. Understanding the techniques means that we can all be wiser consumers, more aware citizens, and better students and teachers.

Chapter 7: Now What?

We have learned about the brain. We have learned about the history of psychology as a field. We have explored the history and use of mind-reading, hypnosis, deception, neuro-linguistic programming and covert neuro-linguistic programming, also known as conversational hypnosis. How can you use these skills and techniques in both your personal and professional life?

How Are These Skills and Strategies Used in Personal and Professional Situations?

In both the personal and professional arenas, mind-reading, hypnosis, deception and neuro-linguistic programming (covert and open) are used to bring about behaviors or behavioral changes in others or oneself.

In your personal life, these techniques or strategies have two sets of uses: personal self-improvement or change and impacting the behavior of other people. In impacting the behavior of others, it may be that you are trying to change or motivate behavior in your life partner, children, siblings, parents or friends.

Let's start with the self-improvement aspect of these techniques. Practicing the self-regulation skills and strategies needed to read minds or hypnotize others is helpful in promoting your own health and in helping you to overcome negative behaviors that may impact it. Meditation, controlled breathing practices, mindfulness, and connecting with your inner emotions all are good in terms of stress-reduction, better sleep, lowering blood pressure, and better health outcomes overall. Many medical establishments now offer mindfulness sessions as part of preventive medical care, showing their belief in the benefits. They are also widely used in treatment programs for chronic or terminal illness.

Taking it a step further, learning how to self-hypnotize also positively impacts your physical and mental health. For example, if you are terrified of needles but have a medical condition requiring you to regularly have many shots or infusions, learning to self-hypnotize allows you to move yourself into that relaxed state where the needles aren't as scary. Afraid of take-offs and landings on a plane? Self-hypnotize yourself so they are just part of the journey; not cause for cold sweat. Most children are born with the ability to self-hypnotize without realizing cognitively what they are doing, but many of us lose that ability as we age and as we have more and more stressors and external stimuli in our lives. Getting back to the ability to self-soothe and make ourselves feel safe is a gift, not only to ourselves, but also to others.

What about mind-reading in your own self-care? While mind-reading is trying to understand the thinking of others, if you have the skills and empathy needed to do that for someone else, you are more in tune with your own inner workings, which leads to more personal self-reflection and true understanding of personal motivation and behaviors.

Deception of self? Many people practice small daily deceptions of self as a way to survive or behave in their daily lives. For example, many people set their clocks ten minutes earlier than the correct time so that they will be on-time. That is a deception of oneself that leads to positive behaviors. However, many other ways of practicing self-deception are harmful. Weight? Blood pressure? Substance abuse? These are ways in which humans tell themselves that they aren't struggling as much as they truly are, and therefore, overall deception of oneself is detrimental to their health.

Many medical doctors are now using mental health screening as a way to look at whether someone is struggling and also to double-check on self-deception. Someone who insists that they don't drink alcohol when asked but shows severe liver damage may be self-deceiving, and the concern needs to be addressed. Doctors are also recording the deceptive answers and following up on these issues in subsequent appointments.

NLP for self? Again, understanding how our own minds work and how behavior and emotion are connected allows for stronger self-reflection and personal growth.

What about using these techniques in your personal life with friends or family? Again, focusing on empathy and empathic intuition makes you a better spouse, parent or child. Being able to recognize and understand the emotions and thought process of others also lessens the likelihood of interpersonal disconnects and conflict. Understanding the theory of the inner mental maps of NLP lets you understand how the maps of others impact their reality and, therefore, their behavior. You can use that understanding to motivate and change behavior.

Visualize yourself with your life partner. For the last six months, your partner has come home from work daily with endless complaints about their job and colleagues. Nothing seems to make them happy at work. Using the empathic listening and observation of mind-reading, you don't interject suggestions or comments; you listen and look for the true root of the concerns. Using the hypnosis steps, you help your partner reach a relaxed state in which they can think about the issues and propose their own solutions. Using the mental map methodology of NLP, you can guide them to think of their professional goals and the maps of those who have achieved those goals, and align those new maps for a course of action. In this combined model, your partner feels your love and support, without feeling that you told them what to do. Active listening, empathy and skills to guide them to a relaxed and focused state will all help your relationship.

Visualize yourself as a parent. Your teen is showing behaviors that are not normal or typical for her. The skills and strategies you have learned in this book will show you how to focus on your child, actively listen, help her identify what is impacting her behavior, and help her achieve her goals. If your child is applying to college or for a job, being able to guide them through the process of self-identifying skills, goals and possible barriers is priceless.

Deception? Many parents use deception frequently with their offspring. Cookies? Your son wants cookies as a snack, and as a parent, you say you are out of cookies but have apples, even though you know you tucked away the cookies in the bread box so no one would find them. Santa Claus? Parents tell their children that Santa is watching them in order to motivate better behavior in the holiday season. Are these deceptions harmful? The figurative jury of psychologists has not consistently agreed on the impact of these deceptions. Certainly, good nutrition is imperative to overall health, so limiting cookies is a good thing. But instead of deception, could it be done through open and honest communication about nutrition? What if the child is hurt when he finds out you lied about the cookies? Yes, that could be harmful. Or even worse, the child finds you shoving cookies in your mouth after your deception, and the ramifications of both the deception and you having treats after he had an apple, yes, that would likely have a negative impact on the relationship. Santa? Most psychologists agree that deception carries the positive impact of believing in a magical existence.

Deception with your life partner? Yes, there are some positive uses of deception, such as not telling them what you got them as a birthday gift so that it can be a surprise. Otherwise, deception with your partner leads to the thought process that if you can lie about small things, you might be keeping more harmful secrets from them — like having an affair. In your long-term love relationships, be judicious in your use of deception.

In your work life, many of these skills and techniques have uses for motivating yourself and others. For example, learning empathic listening skills and improving your observation of non-verbal cues will help you to be a better colleague, employee or supervisor. Understanding where behavior and emotions develop and how they manifest will help you better motivate and support those around you at work. While these skills are exceedingly important as an employer, they also are incredibly important as an employee because learning to read the non-verbal cues of a supervisor or boss can be the difference between career advancement and stagnation.

As noted earlier, the practices used in mind-reading and hypnosis are, overall, positive interpersonal skills. They allow you to more deeply connect with other people, and therefore guide and motivate them more fully. Using those skills either directly or covertly will help motivate and inspire those with whom you work. Overall, even using covert NLP should have positive outcomes within the workplace, as it is tapping into the inner motivation of others and helping use that to move an organization or particular project forward.

Again, as noted, deception in the workplace can have very clear benefits in the short term. Sales can be increased, employees motivated to work harder, workplace conflict avoided, and employers feel that they're being supportive. However, when the deception comes to light, it may cause negative outcomes overall. The trust needed in truly successful professional environments will be eroded, and it is likely that your company or organization will get a reputation for subterfuge and dishonesty. Think of companies such as Volkswagen, which faced international condemnation when it was found that they knowingly practiced deception with regards to the emissions of their vehicles. The fall-out from that deceit continues to impact their bottom line as a company several years after it happened, making it a cautionary tale.

Ethical Dilemmas in Using Skills and Strategies

Is it morally and ethically right to use these techniques? If so, when and how?

Research on the effectiveness of the skills and strategies shows that mind-reading, hypnosis and neuro-linguistic programming improve when the subject knows what is going on, is a willing participant, and has goals towards which they want to work. Humans like to self-improve, and overall, they like to help support the goals of others or organizations. When someone knows the how and the why with regard to something they are doing, especially if the person feels valued and supported, they will usually join in the process with an open heart and enthusiasm.

Deception in and of itself can't be openly practiced; after all, if you tell someone you're lying to them from the beginning, you aren't going to be able to deceive them. Therefore, it is an inherently secretive process, so the reason for using it needs to be clear and worth the possible negative outcomes if discovered.

In using these techniques, the ethical question that needs to be answered is whether the desired outcome is worth the effort of the process, and if it is done in secret, is there likely to be such fallout that it would no longer be worthwhile? If it is truly worth the effort, and the risk of negative consequences is low, then it is right to use the techniques.

What Outcomes Can Be Hoped for in Using Skills and Strategies?

In your personal life, using the techniques on yourself, you can expect to be more relaxed, focused, and better able to achieve your goals. These strategies can improve attention and organization, increase creativity, and lead to a sense of greater calm and focus.

In a professional setting, you can improve the functionality of your team, increase productivity, and depending on the techniques you are using, increase the overall sense of safety, security and value. Employees and employers are more productive and motivated when they feel understood and valued, have an understanding of a common goal, and know the plan to achieve the goal, whether it is a personal or professional goal or the goal of the organization.

Why Would Anyone Use These Skills and Strategies?

Now that you know about these skills, why would you use them? First, these are skills that anyone can learn to use. You don't need an advanced degree or a specialist to come into your home or workspace to implement them. You don't need to announce their use, and you can pick and choose pieces of them as they fit into your life or practice.

The skills of empathic and active listening and the observation of non-verbal cues all help you get along better with the people in your life. Adding in the techniques that allow you to focus on goals and how to achieve them is motivational, and the use of inner mapping can help anyone visualize and move toward those goals.

Chapter 8: Using These Techniques Well in Your Own Life

As we have briefly looked at using mind-reading, hypnosis, deception, and open and covert neuro-linguistic programming in both personal and professional settings, it is time to focus more fully on a step-by-step approach to using them in your own personal life.

How, Where, When and Why to Use Skills and Strategies in Your Life

You know how to read minds. You know how to self-hypnotize or hypnotize others. You know how to use deception. And you understand the principles of neuro-linguistic programming when used both openly and covertly. How do you use them to your best advantage in your own life?

Start with learning the mindfulness techniques used in both mind-reading and hypnosis. Find a quiet, comfortable spot to sit. Sit in a position that works for your body in terms of comfort but is not too comfortable. Make sure there are no distractions in the room, such as a phone that might ring or a television that is on. If you have pets, it is a good time to have your pets be in another room so they don't decide that it's the perfect time to climb on your lap for snuggles. Sit with your back straight, and breathe in through your nose, filling your lungs with air. Hold. Release it, exhaling through your mouth. Repeat the process. After several repetitions, close your eyes.

Focus on the feeling of the air moving in through your nostrils. Focus on what your lungs and rib-cage feel like when your lungs are fully inflated. Keep breathing in through your nose and out through your mouth, and let your mind focus on the rhythm of your breaths.

Then focus on relaxing each and every inch of your body, starting with your toes and moving up to the top of your head. If you move past an area of the body and later feel it tensing, go back to that point and repeat the process. If you feel tension, focus on letting that muscle open up, welcoming it to sink into your chair. As you breathe and release your physical tension, let your mind wander to what is making you tense. Is that neck-pain and tension because you slept wrong when you curled up with your daughter on the couch the evening before, or is it because you are concerned about a work issue? Understand what is causing your tension.

Then, regardless of whether or not you plan to use mind-reading, hypnosis, deception or neuro-linguistic programming, whether formally or informally, welcome in their focus on how humans react to things, what we can learn by observing the non-verbal responses of ourselves and others, and how we can use that knowledge to achieve our personal and professional goals.

For example, understanding that your employer shows his happiness through non-verbal cues like whistling show tunes gives you a read on his emotional state when you go in for a high-stakes meeting. You get up on the morning of that meeting, practice your mindfulness meditation so that your mind and body are as relaxed and focused as they can be. Then, heading into his office, you hear him whistling a song from Oklahoma. You know he is in a good mood, which means he is more open to out-of-the-box suggestions, and you go in and hit a home run with your new idea.

Or the flip side: you know that your mother-in-law pinches the bridge of her nose when she is getting angry about something, even if she continues to smile and say everything is fine. Sitting at the table in a restaurant, you watch as her eyes keep darting to your spouse, who keeps pouring and drinking more wine. Your mother-in-law starts pinching her nose, and you know that any second, there will be an eruption. Quietly, you slide the wine bottle away from your spouse, and when the waiter asks if your table would like more wine, you say no. Problem averted.

Maybe you want a change of career. For as long as you can remember, you have wanted to be a fashion designer. You went to a great art school, and after graduating, you applied for every job you could in the field and didn't get a single call back. Years of working dull office jobs has left you sad and bitter, disillusioned at best. Taking the steps to learn about reading your own body and mind, you realize that you need to get back to the creative side of yourself, and you work with a neuro-linguistic programming practitioner, who helps you understand your own inner mental map of who you are and how you fit in the world. That practitioner helps you determine who in the field of fashion you would most like to be like and helps you understand their inner map so that you can follow the same steps to success. Two years of focus and attention to those inner maps, and you have a job in a clothing design company, are being creative again, and are professionally fulfilled and a lot more fun to be around.

Pros and Cons of Using Skills and Strategies

The mind-body connection inherent in mind-reading, hypnosis and neuro-linguistic programming all have strong positive aspects to them. People feel more in control of their lives, understand their motivations, and can avoid pitfalls.

Deception can be wildly effective in helping you achieve your goals, but between the moral considerations and the need to keep any deceptions clear in your own mind, it is likely to eventually add more stress and conflict than it resolves.

Expected Outcomes

Increased understanding of how our own minds and emotions work and knowledge of what we truly want in life — and why we want it — all lead to clearer focus, increased motivation and behavioral control.

Using hypnosis, whether through self-hypnosis or by being hypnotized by a trained practitioner, can also bring about clear and lasting behavioral or health changes. Blood pressure, eating disorders, anxiety, smoking and other issues can be addressed through hypnosis, leading to improved health.

The benefit or outcome of using these techniques is also that you are more likely to talk with others about active listening, empathic intuition and listening, emotions, mind-body connections, mental maps, relaxation, motivation, focus and goal setting. All of these help grow a community in which people are more aware of their own thoughts and emotions, and more aware of and connected to those of others.

Chapter 9: Going Forward

The human brain is an amazing machine. It is not only the seat of our cognition; it is the organ that controls all of our bodily functions and our emotions. We have learned about the history of the study of the brain as an organ and the study of psychology, and we have learned how it has changed over the years.

As part of our study of psychology, we have also learned about mind-reading, hypnosis, deception and neuro-linguistic programming. In regard to NLP, we have learned about using it both openly and covertly. All of these techniques or strategies are used to improve oneself or others and to help move people toward goals, whether their own or those of others.

Summary of New Learning

In the preceding chapters, much information about the brain, psychology, mind-reading, hypnosis, deception and neuro-linguistic programming has been shared. To recap, mind-reading is much more than an entertainer standing on stage and making educated guesses about members of the audience. It is not the sharing of messages from a departed loved one. It is the combination of empathic and active listening, reading of non-verbal cues, and reading the body language of the subject. It also involves being able to focus fully on another human being, without distraction, so that you can truly observe their reactions. Put it all together, and you will read the mind of another person.

As a reminder of the steps discussed earlier, this is what you need to do in order to read someone's mind:

- Step one: Decide who you want to read and why. What are you trying to learn from the person?

- Step two: Be aware of your own mind-body connection. Practice your own mindfulness. As discussed previously, if you aren't centered yourself, you won't be able to tune in to the feelings of others.

- Step three: Truly focus on the person you plan to read. Reflect on everything you have ever noticed about the person. What triggers them? What makes them laugh? What non-verbal cues do they give when agitated or in an emotional state? How do they act when calm and happy?

- Step four: Find a distraction-free environment in which to read the person's mind, and then make eye contact for 15 seconds.

- Step five: Start a conversation, moving from fixed answer questions to open-ended ones, reading their reactions and establishing rapport.

- Step six: Move toward the topic you want to know about, and begin to ask questions or invite conversation about it.

- Step seven: Intuit their thoughts on the topic based on their reactions to the conversation.

- Follow-up: Use the information you gleaned toward accomplishing your goal.

Hypnosis has more of a scientific background, and therefore now has more of an accepted role in psychology and medicine. In hypnosis, the subject is guided to a deeply relaxed state in which they are more responsive to suggestions from the hypnotist and more able to focus on how to solve problems or change their behavior. While hypnosis also has a long tradition of being used in entertainment, it has a growing collection of data to support its use in treating mental health and other health issues such as anxiety, smoking and overeating.

In summary, the steps to openly hypnotize someone are:

- Step one: Determine who you want to hypnotize and why you want to hypnotize them. Make sure the person is not mentally ill and does not have a history of trauma.

- Step two: Both of you move to a quiet, distraction-free environment.

- Step three: Have the subject sit or lie down comfortably.

- Step four: Review the process and clarify goals.

- Step five: Start speaking to the person in a consistently calm and relaxing tone of voice.

- Step six: Instruct the subject to focus on taking deep regular breaths and model the breathing pattern for them.

- Step seven: Instruct the subject to focus their eyes on a fixed point.

- Step eight: Guide the subject through a systematic pattern of body relaxation, moving from the toes to the top of the head.

- Step nine: Guide the subject down a figurative staircase with verbal directions.

- Step ten: Work on the goals established prior to the session.

- Step eleven: Bring the subject out of the hypnotic state.

- Step twelve: Discuss and reflect on the process.

To self-hypnotize, the steps are:

- Step one: Move to a quiet, distraction-free environment.

- Step two: Sit or lie down comfortably.

- Step three: Focus on taking deep regular breaths in through the nose and out through the mouth, holding them in between.

- Step four: Follow a systematic pattern of body relaxation, moving from the toes to the top of the head.

- Step five: Work on your goals.

- Step six: Bring yourself back to the present slowly.

What about when you want to hypnotize someone without their knowledge? The steps are:

- Step one: As with open hypnosis, determine who you want to hypnotize, and determine why you want to do it. Make sure the person is not mentally ill and does not have a history of trauma.

- Step two: Both of you move to a quiet, distraction-free environment if possible.

- Step three: Have the subject sit comfortably.

- Step four: Start speaking to the person in a consistently calm and relaxing tone of voice.

- Step five: Model deep breathing without mentioning that you're doing it. The subject is likely to align their breathing with yours without realizing it.

- Step six: Use open-ended questions to open the subject's brain to your suggestions.

- Step seven: Work on the goals you established through gentle suggestions.

- Step eight: Bring the subject out of the hypnotic state.

- Step nine: Process and reflect on the hypnosis when the subject leaves the room.

- Step ten (long-term): Continue the process regularly until the goal is achieved.

In deception, the person practicing the deception gives misleading, incomplete or untrue information in order to bring about a specific behavioral response in the subject. For example, saying that Santa won't come unless the playroom is clean has motivated many children. In the workplace, saying that the supervisor is unhappy with an employee when that isn't the case will motivate the employee to go overboard in trying to please the boss.

How do you practice deception?

- Step one: Determine the goal of your deception and who you plan to deceive, and come up with a plan of how to either withhold information or share incorrect or misleading information.

- Step two: Follow your outlined plan.

- Step three: Make sure to keep the truth and the deception clear in your own mind so as to not cause confusion or mistakes.

- Step four: Use the resulting behaviors of the person or persons deceived to move toward your goal.

- Step five: Determine follow-up steps.

Neuro-linguistic programming takes the understanding of verbal and non-verbal communication stressed by mind-reading, combines it with the deeply relaxed and focused state of hypnosis, and adds to it the idea of a personal inner map of your beliefs and goals. It helps you to take your own mental map and superimpose it over the map of someone you admire, and follow the steps they did to hopefully achieve the same outcome.

For example, if you want to be a newspaper journalist, learning about the mental map of the greatest reporters and how they achieved their success will allow you to understand how to follow in their footsteps. Covert NLP is using the same ideas but working without the subject's knowledge or permission. Covert NLP is also often referred to as conversational hypnosis, as it relies on getting past someone's defenses to their true thoughts, feelings and goals.

To practice NLP covertly, use the steps for mind-reading after clearly understanding both your own goals and the inner mental map of the subject. Then use the steps of hypnosis to start planting the suggestions that will merge your goals into the maps of others.

- Step one: Be mindful of your own body and emotions.

- Step two: Understand your own inner mental map, including your own goals, and how you plan to reach those goals.

- Step three: Pick your subject for the process.

- Step four: Determine how that subject can help you achieve your goals or the goals you have for that person.

- Step five: Invite the person to a distraction-free environment.

- Step six: Use your mind-reading and hypnosis skills to understand their motivations and emotions and also get them into a suggestible state of mind.

- Step seven: Start planting suggestions of how they can change their behavior in such a way as to help you achieve the goals you have set.

- Step eight (long-term): Continue to repeat the process, guiding the subject along the clear steps to achieve the goals.

Summary of How to Use the Skills and Strategies

These skills and strategies can be used both on yourself and others, or you can also choose to seek a professional practitioner to support you in using them for your own personal growth.

Mind-reading should be used with people you know or have a connection to or a reason to try to know them well. It involves focusing fully on another, listening to words, observing actions, observing their non-verbal cues and communication, and understanding possible motivations for that person. Use it to help you understand why people do the things they do, especially if you are using it to try to improve or change the behaviors of someone for the better. If you are an employer and you know that one of your employees doesn't get along with others, use your mind-reading abilities to understand exactly what is going on with that person and help move them forward and work with colleagues in a healthier manner.

Hypnosis involves guiding oneself or others to a state of full relaxation and safety where the person is more open to suggestions and better able to problem solve in that state. People in a hypnotic state are better able to focus on a problem or negative behavior. They are more able to solve it creatively and are open to suggestions of the hypnotist about changing the behavior.

Without formal training as a clinical psychologist and hypnotherapist, hypnosis should not be used to address past trauma or recover repressed memories. In the home or workplace, hypnosis, practiced both openly and covertly, can be used to help with interpersonal relationships, anxiety and stress, and overall fears. As a parent, teaching your child how to self-hypnotize and understand what it is and why they are doing it is a gift, as it will help them self-manage and regulate their emotions.

Deception is the action of telling or sharing incomplete, incorrect or misleading information in order to achieve a specific goal, such as managing the behavior of a child, motivating employees to work harder and better, or convincing an employee to leave the company.

The recommendation with regards to using deception is to first make sure that if you are practicing it, you maintain a clear view of the truth. Second, make sure that you keep the deception clear in your own mind so that you don't ruin your effort by slipping up with your lie. Third, make sure to use deception judiciously. If it is your go-to technique as partner, employer or employee, you should think about whether the relationship or job is right for you. Finally, make sure that if your deception is uncovered, your reason for doing it in the first place is so strong that there is the possibility of retaining the relationship if you want to do so.

Neuro-linguistic programming uses the same ideas of deep relaxation, focus, and the reading of verbal communication and non-verbal cues as both mind-reading and hypnosis does. It then takes it a step further, asking the subject (if practiced openly) to focus on their inner mental map of their own reality; then to assess their own personal goals or the goals of a particular group or organization. Then the subject is guided to learn about and understand successful communicators and high-achievers in the same field to understand how they achieved their goals. Use of visualization and structured learning allows the subject to understand the process and then follow the new inner mental map to achieve the set goals.

Practiced covertly, neuro-linguistic programming uses the same knowledge of the subject or subjects, and it can be used in large groups in what is called conversational hypnosis. In conversational hypnosis, the subject or subjects are guided unknowingly to a feeling or emotion about a particular event or goal. The practitioner guides them, without their knowledge, to a shared understanding or a shared emotional state; then to a shared goal and a shared course of action relating to that goal.

Can you impact your personal and professional life by using these techniques? Can you be more successful as a leader? Will using them improve your personal relationships? Yes, you can both curry favor and achieve positive outcomes by using these techniques, and doing so is not expensive or even terribly time consuming.

Why do they work? How does using them help with relationships and, therefore, with outcomes? Being able to truly focus on another person, to listen to them actively, and to be observant of their non-verbal behaviors is helpful in relationships, whether at work or in our families. That gift of full focus on another is truly wonderful and increasingly rare in our more and more technologically advanced and dependent world. Our colleagues, customers, employers and employees all appreciate feeling that they are important enough for us to take the time to talk to without distraction and to be aware of their likes and dislikes and their inner motivation. When we are using our skills of mind-reading and covert hypnosis, the subjects may not know they are being handled or impacted, but usually, one outcome is the person feeling the practitioner truly cares.

Open hypnosis is unlikely to be practiced in many work environments, unless it is being done formally through some sort of initiative or employee assistance program, and open hypnosis in the workplace without proper training and licensure could lead to significant liability issues. However, in our family lives, we can use hypnotism as a way to help with stress, anxiety and insomnia. It can also be used to help loved ones focus on goals and dreams. Of course, we can all practice self-hypnotism. Being able to guide ourselves to a state of inner calmness and focus through self-hypnosis means that we are more likely to be able to reduce stress, achieve our own goals and help others achieve theirs.

Neuro-linguistic programming is likely the technique that will create the most lasting impact and change in a work environment if practiced openly, ethically, and with fidelity. Using the explanation of the success of others as a map and overlaying it with our own inner maps and the institutional goals of a company or organization can lead to huge growth in success.

How to Continue Your Learning on These Topics

There are many outstanding how-to books and videos to learn about these topics in even more detail, including step-by-step pictorial explanations on them.

For hypnosis, if your goal is to use it for more than just reducing stress and increasing focus and motivation, seek a professional training program where your learning and progress are monitored. Due to the possibility of triggering trauma responses or scratching the surface of hidden memories, it is imperative that hypnosis be practiced with integrity and control.

If you are interested in further learning about the use of deception as a tool, there are many studies of the uses and impacts that can be found through an Internet search. If you are an employer or supervisor, consider also learning about how to detect deception in others and how deception on the part of your employees can impact the overall climate of a work environment.

For neuro-linguistic programming, in order to learn the full power of the practice, you should join a group that studies and practices it in order to observe how other practitioners help a subject understand their inner map and goals. Again, if done well, it can be hugely impactful for someone in understanding their goals and working toward them, but with someone especially vulnerable, doing it poorly can lead to problems with self-esteem and mental health.

There are many outstanding resources about these topics online, including many videos and tutorials on how to practice the skills, as well as information about empirical data on their use and effectiveness.

Other ways to learn about these techniques? Advanced study in the fields of psychology, education and marketing often have classes or workshops where these techniques are used, where you can be trained in person or online by experts who have years of experience and can also help with guidance on ethics and effectiveness in various situations.

A Call to Action to Use Them for Positive Growth

The techniques of mind-reading, hypnosis, deception and open and covert neuro-linguistic programming as tools in both our personal and professional lives is clear. They can be powerful tools, both for good or bad purposes and outcomes.

Encouraging your child toward good behavior by deception about Santa, as long as the child has strong self-esteem overall, is not likely to psychologically scar them. Telling your child that they were not adopted when they were, however, is likely to have a scarring effect. Telling your boss that she is a strong leader when she isn't is likely to curry you favor and likely won't hurt others. On the other hand, telling your boss that another employee talks about her behind her back in a detrimental way when it is not true is likely to cause negative fallout all around. Use the power wisely and for the right reasons.

Mind-reading, hypnosis and neuro-linguistic programming all stress the idea of a deep understanding of the motivations of others, their emotions, their non-verbal cues, and their ultimate goals. That level of understanding of others and the empathy involved in such knowledge can have huge positive power. Again, use the power wisely.

All of these techniques should be used with extreme care with children, making sure that they have the emotional strength and knowledge to use these skills and learning well. These techniques should not be used with anyone particularly vulnerable or mentally ill without full training and support. Using these techniques to treat mental illness or medical ailments or to deal with past traumas should never be done without the correct medical and psychological training.

Learning about other humans, truly listening to them with an open heart and mind, reading their body language and non-verbal cues, and helping them achieve specific goals can be incredibly powerful for practitioners and can lead to great good.

Use your new-found knowledge and skills for positive reasons: use them to improve your personal and/or professional world and therefore make the entire world better for every person.

Conclusion

The human brain is the seat of all human reason and emotion. All bodily responses are controlled by the various lobes of the human brain. Every human needs to understand the different parts of the brain and how they control every aspect of our lives. There are techniques that can be used to improve our own responses and behaviors, as well as changing and improving the behavior and responses of others. Understanding the roles of thought, emotion and motivation can help us motivate both ourselves and others.

The Growth and Changes in Psychology

You have learned extensively about the human brain, the approximately three pounds of matter that controls bodily functions, emotions, thoughts, and every other part of keeping us alive. You've learned how the brain works and how humans have worked for centuries to try to understand how to change human behavior. You have learned that the human brain can be injured and still function. You know now that the human brain is a highly complex organism, divided into separate lobes or sections: the brain stem, the cerebellum, the occipital lobe, the parietal lobe, the temporal lobe and the frontal lobe. The understanding of the human brain and the ways in which the brain controls both the body and emotion is still largely a mystery, and the base of knowledge about these topics grows daily.

As we have learned, psychology is a very complex discipline that has only really been around since the late 1800s. Early philosophers pondered behavior and emotion but attributed them to many different factors, such as astrological influences or spirits. Many people were treated horribly or even killed because of beliefs that evil spirits were guiding their behavior rather than a desire to understand that there might be another explanation for what was happening behaviorally.

The accident of Phinneas Gage forced doctors and scientists to try to understand how an injury to the brain could impact personality, and in doing so, the mind-body-emotion-behavior connections became more and more clear. Gage showed that different parts of the brain control different parts of thinking, speaking, bodily functions and emotions. After learning about the importance of Gage, we saw how psychology continued to shift its theories, arriving at cognitive psychology, which has led to the counseling and behavioral response approaches we see most frequently now.

Mind-reading, hypnosis, deception and neuro-linguistic programming are all examples of ways in which the mind and body connect and the ways in which human behavior can be understood and impacted by suggestion. The techniques we have explored help us to access the control center for thought, emotion and motivation in others. Mind-reading, hypnosis, deception and neuro-linguistic programming are all techniques used to understand human emotions, thought and behavior.

At their heart, all of these techniques have the common purpose of looking to change, motivate or manipulate the behavior of oneself or others. By learning the techniques, we learn more about how our brains work and also focus more fully on how to work with others. Each of these techniques involve an understanding of oneself and others and an understanding of the goals we each have. They can be used to help move our own personal agendas forward, or they can be used to work within and advance the progress of organizations or companies.

The techniques used primarily in mind-reading, hypnosis and neuro-linguistic programming all use empathy, observation and understanding of verbal and non-verbal communication, understanding of human motivation, systems theory and interpersonal skills as a basis. All of them can help us to understand ourselves and others better, and as leaders and employers, can help us to motivate our staff to achieve their greatest potential. Deception can also be used to motivate behavior and may have positive outcomes for those practicing it, although its use continues to be controversial. Deception also can potentially be problematic if the deceit is uncovered, whereas the other techniques, if used covertly, aren't as likely to inspire anger if detected.

Your Learning and Moving Forward

Take your knowledge of the skills of mind-reading, hypnosis, deception and both open and covert neuro-linguistic programming, and decide how best to use them in your personal and professional life. Learn the skills of active and empathic listening; learn to read non-verbal skills; practice focusing on other people in locations or situations in which you can fully focus on them without distraction. Learn how to use these skills to improve your own productivity and mental health, while not using them in a way that is harmful to others. Make sure that if you are using these skills on others, your subject is not vulnerable, fragile or damaged, and ensure that they don't have significant mental health issues. Make sure that you are not impacting the physical health of someone who has a health issue by convincing them that your skills will cure them in some way.

Mind-reading, hypnosis, deception and open and covert neuro-linguistic programming can all help you and others achieve set goals and change behaviors. They can help you address your own issues and behaviors and help you move toward achieving your own goals. They can help you move others toward their goals and toward supporting you in reaching your personal goals and your organization's goals. They are powerful, potentially life-changing tools. Use them well!

References

Grinder, J. & Bandler, R. (1976). The Structure of Magic. Palo Alto (Calif.): Science and Behavior Books.

Hunter, R. (2010). The Art of Hypnotherapy. Bancyfelin: Crown House Publishing.

Mann, S. (2016). Psychology: A Complete Introduction. London: John Murray Learning.

Navarro, J. & Karlins, M. (2015). What Every Body is Saying: An Ex-Fbi Agent's Guide to Speed-Reading People. New York, NY: Harper Collins.

www.ingramcontent.com/pod-product-compliance
Lightning Source LLC
Chambersburg PA
CBHW050734030426
42336CB00012B/1553